W9-BYV-213

ADVANCE PRAISE FOR *YOU. ARE. THE. ONE.* BY KUTE BLACKSON

"*You. Are. The. One.* is filled with wonderful stories and simple, powerful information. Kute Blackson is a strong heart, wise soul, and bold truth teller. This book doesn't stop giving, and neither does he."

—Marianne Williamson, #1 *New York Times* bestselling author of *A Return to Love* and *Everyday Grace*

"*You. Are. The. One.* is a very powerful book that will help you remember who you really are. Kute Blackson brilliantly guides you beyond any limiting stories and teaches you the priceless secrets to freedom. This book is fuel for your soul."

—Don Miguel Ruiz, bestselling author of *The Four Agreements*

"Kute Blackson is a leading visionary in the field of personal development. His work is remarkable, powerful, and will transform your life. *You. Are. The. One.* is a must read for all!!"

—Larry King, Emmy- and Peabody-winning talk-show host

"Kute Blackson's *You. Are. The. One.* is a wise compass for the soul, pointing us in the direction of the innermost fulfillment of the human spirit. The true-life stories of personal triumph he shares are touched with heaven's kiss of inspiration. Let his compassionate teachings bless your heart."

—Michael Bernard Beckwith, author of *Spiritual Liberation* and *Life Visioning*

"Kute Blackson is a bold voice and leader for the new generation of seekers. His book *You. Are. The. One.* is a unique message that will inspire you to fulfill your full potential and create the life you want!"

—Jack Canfield, author of *The Success Principles* and co-creator of the #1 *New York Times* bestselling *Chicken Soup for the Soul* series

"Kute Blackson is the real deal. His book *You. Are. The. One.* will take you on a profound journey of self-discovery, and powerfully guide you to step into your greatness. He reminds you of the innate power you possess. This book is a bold wake-up call to living your destiny!"

—John Gray, author of the *New York Times* bestseller *Men Are from Mars, Women Are from Venus*

"*You. Are. The. One.* is not your average self-help book, and Kute Blackson is not your average person! Kute possesses a special gift that was passed down to him from his ancestors. He offers his deep wisdom in this book in a way that's easy to read and absorb. *You. Are. The. One.* will challenge you to go beyond your limitations and help you reconnect with your soul!"

—Marci Shimoff, #1 *New York Times* bestselling author of *Happy for No Reason*

"Kute Blackson is a passionate visionary whose inspiration, wisdom, and heart will infuse your own transformational journey with renewed purpose. His book will ignite you and uplift you."

—Dr. Barbara De Angelis, #1 NY Times bestselling author of *Soul Shifts*

"Kute Blackson is a modern-day mystic who truly walks his talk. In *You. Are. The. One.* he shares his deepest love, wisest wisdom, and mesmerizing, transformative stories, which provide everything you need to know to live life fully."

—Arielle Ford, author of *Turn Your Mate into Your Soulmate*

"Again and again through each compelling story, I became Kute's student, his peer, and finally his brother. Great teachers know how to pace their revelations to defeat our resistance as they reveal the truth. Kute Blackson is among the greatest."

—Mike Dooley, *New York Times* bestselling author of *Infinite Possibilities* and *Leveraging the Universe*

"Kute Blackson has written an inspirational classic that will give you the keys you need in order to reclaim your power and create the life that you have always dreamed about! Once you read *You. Are. The. One.* you will have no more excuses. Kute Blackson is a gifted guide and a unique voice of inspiration for today's times."

—Lisa Nichols, *New York Times* bestselling author of *No Matter What!*

"Kute Blackson is wise, courageous, profound, and unstoppable when it comes to stripping us of everything in the way of true personal power. This man is ruthless at getting to the truth, and the journey of reading this powerhouse of a book is one of deep truth telling and audacious awakening. Read it at your own risk! I promise you won't be the same person you are now when you've finished, but a more expanded, creatively alive, and awake version of yourself! The person that you were born to become!"

—Katherine Woodward Thomas, *New York Times* bestselling author of *Calling in "The One"* and *Conscious Uncoupling*

"Kute Blackson is a remarkable man. He is a wonderful exception in a world overpopulated by pundits and politicians telling us how to live while not walking their talk. He lives the principles offered in the pages of this compelling book. You can trust this book to enrich your life."

—Stewart Emery, co-author of *Success Built to Last* and first CEO of est and cofounder of Actualizations

"When you read a book like this, there are the words, and then there is where the words are coming from. These days, we are bombarded with words. It's raining, hailing words, in every possible medium. What you hold here in your hands is a precious jewel because of the source from where the words come. I have gotten to know Kute Blackson quite well over the last years, and I know something of the extraordinary story of his life. This is a man of reliable integrity, ruthless honesty, and endlessly generous compassion. Don't pass your soul around casually to strangers. Think carefully before you trust someone to guide you deeper into yourself. Kute is a man I have frequently turned to myself for guidance and reflection. I wholeheartedly encourage you to extend to him the same trust."

—Arjuna Ardagh, founder of Awakening Coaching and co-author of *Conscious Men, Better than Sex,* and *The Translucent Revolution*

"*You. Are. The. One.* takes you on the adventure of a lifetime into the deepest recesses of your soul. There you find unconditional love, compassion, joy, God, abiding peace, timeless wisdom, and personal power. I immediately ordered ten copies for the people I love most! This book will change your life."

—Raz Ingrasci, teacher and coach and chairman of the Hoffman Institute International

"What you are holding in your hands is an adventure journal, a self-help tool kit, and spiritual credo in one power-packed book. Kute is an expert at stripping away anything that no longer serves you and giving you the tools, and inspiration, to rebuild your faith in yourself while showing you how to live a bigger life, a more true life, a more YOU life. I couldn't put it down."

—Rhonda Britten, Emmy Award–winner,
author, and founder of Fearless Living

"Kute Blackson opens a solid, in-your-face dialogue about a very important subject . . . ourselves. And he does so by masterfully combining ancient wisdom with present-day techniques. He is totally committed, and will go to any extreme necessary in order to transform. *You. Are. The. One.* is a very disruptive but tremendously loving and effective guide. He is a much needed, fresh voice in the already crowded, self-discovery scene. Kute Blackson is spirituality 2.0."

—Pepe Aguilar, nine-time Grammy winner,
singer, songwriter, and producer

"*You. Are. The. One.* is a guided journey to the center of your soul. Kute Blackson shares with us ancient truths in a language we can all understand." —LeVar Burton, actor, director, and author of *Aftermath*

"Every now and again a book comes along that is a game changer. *You. Are. The. One.* is one of those! Kute Blackson has a unique way of teaching that will engage your soul and deeply transform your life. The wisdom in this book is universal and timeless. No matter who you are, it will deliver to you what you most need!"

—Adam Markel, author of *Pivot* and CEO of New Peaks

"Kute Blackson has mastered the art of transforming lives and will help you transform yours. *You. Are. The. One.* will take you on a radical journey where you'll have the opportunity to plumb the depths of your soul while also learning tools for manifesting your dreams. No small feat."

—H. Ronald Hulnick, president of the University
of Santa Monica and co-author of
Loyalty to Your Soul: The Heart of Spiritual Psychology

NORTH
STAR
WAY

A BOLD ADVENTURE IN FINDING PURPOSE, DISCOVERING THE REAL YOU, AND LOVING FULLY

Kute Blackson

New York London Toronto Sydney New Delhi

Reader's Note:
This book reflects my experiences over a period of years. Certain names and identifying characteristics have been changed, and certain individuals and events are composites.

North Star Way
An Imprint of Simon & Schuster, Inc.
1230 Avenue of the Americas
New York, NY 10020

First North Star Way hardcover edition June 2016

NORTH STAR WAY and colophon are trademarks of Simon & Schuster, Inc.

For information about special discounts for bulk purchases, please contact Simon & Schuster Special Sales at 1-866-506-1949 or business@simonandschuster.com

The North Star Way Speakers Bureau can bring authors to your live event. For more information or to book an event, contact the North Star Way Speakers Bureau at 1-212-698-8888 or visit our site, thenorthstarway.com.

Interior design by Renato Stanisic

Manufactured in the United States of America

10 9 8 7 6 5 4 3 2 1

Library of Congress Cataloging-in-Publication Data

Names: Blackson, Kute, author.
Title: You are the one : a bold adventure in finding purpose, discovering the real you, and loving fully / by Kute Blackson.
Description: New York : North Star Way, 2016.
Identifiers: LCCN 2016005840 | ISBN 9781501127274 (hardback)
Subjects: LCSH: Self-realization. | Spiritual life. | Conduct of life. | BISAC: SELF-HELP / Motivational & Inspirational. | SELF-HELP / Personal Growth / Happiness. | SELF-HELP / Spiritual.
Classification: LCC BJ1470 .B53 2016 | DDC 204/.4—dc23
LC record available at http://lccn.loc.gov/2016005840

ISBN 978-1-5011-2727-4
ISBN 978-1-5011-2731-1 (ebook)

This book is dedicated to each of YOU who courageously dare to live your truth.

And also to my mother and father. I love you.

CONTENTS

PROLOGUE

THE RICHEST MAN IN THE WORLD

I stepped off the train, the sweat dripping down my face, desperate for some sort of breeze.

There was no relief, just the hot Indian sun blazing down on me from above.

I was so hot, so tired, that I couldn't even figure out where to go. I just needed to sit down and rest.

I collapsed on a bench in front of the Mahabodhi Temple.

I was in Bodhgaya, the town where you can find the tree under which the Buddha attained enlightenment.

But at this point, enlightenment was the last thing on my mind.

I had been in India for weeks and I was desperate for a break. Some air-conditioning. A soft bed. Some peace and quiet.

This bench would have to do.

But as I closed my eyes, I heard music amid the bustling noises of the crowds. Some singing, chanting, and drumming.

I opened my eyes.

Lined up in front of the temple were ten beggars in formation, as if on some kind of beggars' row, bowls in hand. My eyes fell upon one man at the end of the line.

Dressed in a blue wrap and nothing else, the man was drumming to the beat of his song. I could tell his hymns were to God, as he was singing his heart out, eyes closed, face lifted to the heavens. I was entranced. He sang with such devotion, purity, passion, and joy that my exhaustion melted away.

As I sat there watching this man, I soon realized why his eyes were closed. He was blind. This man couldn't see if he was making any money because he had no idea whether anyone was even listening to him.

As I watched him sing with no need for any recognition, I thought of all the things I did in my life, simply in pursuit of money. All the things I did in my life, just to be seen and recognized. This man wasn't singing his song for wealth or fame. His intention seemed to be pure . . . utter devotion.

And then I realized that this beggar had stumps instead of arms. I was shocked. He'd shown such mastery with his drum that I'd failed to notice. Unbelievable.

He can't see!

He has no arms!

He has no hands!

I began to weep, my head in my hands, standing right there in plain view of the other beggars. There was something in his simple devotion, despite all he lacked, that revealed how much I took all of my blessings for granted.

If this guy wanted to moan and complain, I'd certainly understand.

And yet here he was, at peace.

The more I thought about what his life must have been like, the more the tears fell. I thought about how I'd eat if I had no hands. Or how I'd pee. Or how I'd maneuver around the world without sight. In an instant, I saw and felt how very little I'd been appreciating what I had, always thinking there must be something more.

It was at that moment that I realized that this fellow was not running around hustling foreigners like the others. And it wasn't because he couldn't see or use his hands, but because there was something else I'd missed entirely.

This man had no legs.

Okay, I was already a slobbering, sobbing mess, but this truly undid me.

This man with nothing was teaching me everything.

I walked over to this beggar and knelt beside him. I looked at him. He turned and looked right at me. Despite his blindness, I could feel his gaze pierce through me.

I wanted to talk to this man. I wanted to know the secret to his devotion. I looked desperately around for a translator. Finally I found a man who spoke English and pulled him to the beggar's side.

"How do you do it?" I asked. "How do you come out here day in and day out, singing and giving and sharing like this?"

As I waited for the translator to relay my message, I was

expecting the heavens to part and some great esoteric wisdom to pass this man's lips.

The man simply looked at me and with one line like a bullet to my heart said with a smile, "What else is there to do but love?"

Then he looked away and resumed his singing . . . just like that.

I was speechless.

When he finished his song, he looked in my direction again. "Young man," he said, "life might give you what you want. Life may never give you what you want. But you can always give life who you are."

He turned back around and started singing again, as if nothing had happened.

I SAT AND STARED, in awe of the truth of his statement.

Now, perhaps that man had a simpler life than we do. He didn't have hands. He had no legs. He had no sight. So his life could have been very limited.

But in so many ways he was right. We think our lives are about hustling, about doing, about accomplishing. Or when life isn't going well, we think it's about complaining, wallowing in our misery, praying for things to be better.

But that man right there in the heat of India, one with so much "missing" in his life, felt instead like the richest man in the world. And he was going to sing his song to the universe, thanking it for its gifts. Every. Single. Day.

After a while in this man's presence, I knew it was time for me to move on. But before I left, I wanted to give him something, for I knew he had given me one of the greatest lessons of my life. I had reached into my pocket when he stopped singing, turned to me again, and said, "I don't need your money. Just share your gifts with the world." He paused. "Who you are is a gift. By not sharing who you really are with the world, you are robbing them of something they need."

I nodded my head. Again he said with a smile, "What else is there to do?"

As I walked away, I realized I had no more excuses. His lesson couldn't have been more simple or profound. What else is there to do but love, sing your song, and celebrate life?

This book is part of my attempt to do just that.

INTRODUCTION

THE WORLD IS WAITING FOR YOU

No one's coming.

Really.

No. One. Is. Coming.

The government isn't going to save you.

Your parents can't rescue you.

Your friends won't carry you.

No one's coming.

Aren't you tired of waiting? Waiting for someone else to solve your problems? Waiting to be happy? Waiting to feel fulfilled? Waiting to live a life that, deep down, truly feels like the life you want?

I have news for you.

There is no need to wait.

Because YOU are everything you've been looking for.

YOU are the person you have been waiting for.

The world is waiting for . . . YOU.

You. Are. The. One.

Wake-Up Call

This book is an invitation to become like the man in the prologue of this book, whom I call the richest man in the world. No, it's not about riches. It's not about fame. It's about discovering who you really are, and how freeing it can be to share that person with the world. When you know who you truly are and are living the life that you truly want to live, you too can be singing your song, giving your gift, absolutely, completely engaged in the world, every single day.

Do you believe that?

It is possible for all of us. But to be the richest man in the world, you've got to dig deep. You've got to admit to yourself the things that aren't working in your life. You've got to own the truth that you are ready for something more. Sometimes we can't see how we have all the answers we seek because we have been hiding from the truth for so long. We've been living with our head in the sand about the things that aren't working in our lives because we are too scared to move forward.

I know this firsthand. There was a point in my life, as an eighteen-year-old living in London, when I finally dared to start living the life that I wanted: not the life my parents wanted me to live, not the life my peers expected me to pursue, but the life that deep down felt like the life of my wildest dreams. I moved to America. With nothing. Knowing no one. It was one of the craziest things I've ever done.

I had pretended for years that living someone else's life was good enough. Until one day I said to myself, *No more. I'm going to go for it. I get only one life. Life is too short to keep on pretending.*

I listened to my soul. I recognized that I was the only one who could change my life.

It was the best choice I ever made.

What are *you* pretending not to know?

I don't know why I am stuck.

I don't know if this is the right relationship for me.

I don't know what to do.

I call this the "I don't know" game. It's a great way to stay complacent when we fear the unknown.

You see, it's easy to get trapped in the prison of so-called success. You create a life for yourself in the world, and from the outside, it works. You're making money. You have the job, the house, the car. And people are saying, *Look how successful you are. You've got it all. Great job!*

Deep down you know that there is more for you than the life you've created, but it can be hard to sacrifice your neat little life filled with its alluring comforts. But often even when everything is comfortably set up, eventually that comfortable space starts to feel like a prison. In working with thousands of people from around the world, I've seen so many people become focused on getting better prison food rather than on breaking out of prison. Trying to make a small eight-by-eight cell enough for themselves.

The whole world awaits. It's time to break down those bars. They are all an illusion anyway.

So are you ready to stop lying to yourself?

Right now I invite you to become responsible for your life. I invite you to be responsible for your happiness.

No one is coming.

This is not bad news! This is good news! It means you have the power! It means your life is in your hands.

If you feel dissatisfied right now—with life, with love, with money—great! This is a profound moment.

You are outgrowing what has previously worked. You have exhausted one way of doing life. It is a moment for change. It is a moment for reckoning.

To be dissatisfied is to know that you were made for something more.

To be dissatisfied is to listen to the truth that is buried deep within—that you were born for greatness.

Peeling Back to Perfect

When you admit that the way you have been doing things isn't working, then you open yourself up to a new way of living. And in this book I'm going to walk you through a process to get you back in touch with who you truly are. Sometimes we don't even realize how disconnected we can get from our pure essence, but getting back in touch with your soul is what will allow you to start to live a life that finally feels fulfilling. That finally feels free. That finally feels truly powerful.

We've got to peel you back to perfect.

What do I mean? Well, when you were born, you were perfect and free.

If you don't believe me, watch your children or a niece or nephew. Or go to a local park and observe the world of play in front of you. Children are so in touch with their pure essence. They remind us of who we used to be, before we got conditioned to behave a certain way. Before we stopped believing in our dreams. Before we stopped freely expressing ourselves.

Do you remember a moment when you were that free? When you would run up to someone and give him or her a hug? When you knew that you had so much to give the world? You would say, "I love you!" without needing to hear it in return. It just flowed out of you naturally. It wasn't part of a transaction. It was a gift, given freely.

But then life begins to chip away that beautiful, trusting essence. You felt the pain of disappointing your parents over something as simple as getting a B instead of an A on a report card. You felt the heartbreak of your parents getting divorced. Perhaps you experienced a death in the family.

Life happens. And it hurts.

So you learn to go into survival mode. You developed survival mechanisms that prevent you from feeling pain and layer these mechanisms one on top of another to help navigate the world as safely as you can. But those protective layers also cover up that perfect soul that you were born with. Those layers keep you from being who you really are and creating the life that you truly want. You lose touch with the truth that deep down you have everything you need. With the gift you were born to give to the world.

In this book, I'm going to help you peel back those layers

so you can get back in touch with who you truly are. Not who you *think* you are. Not who your parents wanted you to be. Not who your partner is trying to mold you into.

Who you REALLY are.

It's not necessarily an easy process. But it is completely necessary to become truly free.

Over the last decade I have worked with people across the globe, both one-on-one and in small and large auditoriums, helping people transform their lives. All kinds of people. Billionaires. Celebrities. Pop stars. Teenagers. Helping them discover who they really are. Because many times, despite their wealth and "success," they are still completely unsatisfied. In particular, I have taken clients on a completely unconventional, nontraditional transformational experience called the Liberation Experience. It is a fourteen-day, 24/7, nonstop journey through the bowels of India—her slums, sacred sites, and streets teaming with mystery—with one client, and me as their guide.

Now, why would my clients sign up for that?

Doesn't that sound a bit . . . crazy? A little . . . extreme?

You bet. Many of my clients have everything the world tells you will make you a success: They have the perfect family, the important job, the big house, maybe even a private jet. But they don't feel powerful. They aren't happy. They walk through my door to find out why the hell not.

And I take them to India.

We travel to temples. We go running in 114-degree heat. We ride in crazy taxicabs where we fear for our lives.

But we aren't there to be tourists. We aren't there to simply meditate. We aren't there to serve the hundreds of thousands of beggars that line the streets.

We are there to peel back the layers of conditioning—all the roles and responsibilities and fears that they think encompass who they are, so we can reveal who they REALLY are. So they can discover that perfect beautiful, powerful soul that they were born with.

I've now been taking clients for over ten years. And it doesn't disappoint.

This book will take you on a similar journey. No, we aren't going to India. Because through the pages of this book, you will discover . . . you don't need to go to India. To Bali. To yoga. On retreat. On sabbatical. This book will connect you to your real self. This is the REAL journey. It is a journey to show you that deep down, underneath all the ways that you've learned to protect yourself, is your perfect, powerful soul. It is a soul that is infinite. It is a soul that is unique to you. And it is just waiting for you to let it out.

I've seen firsthand people get everything they *thought* they wanted in life and still feel empty. Because if you are not connected to who you REALLY are, what you *think* you want won't be what you *really* want. So it is a fruitless pursuit, chasing and chasing and chasing things that are ultimately meaningless.

This book will help you know what you really, truly want.

The Richest Man in the World

The story that opens this book is about the man I call the richest man in the world.

Why is he the richest man in the world? Because, despite his circumstances, he wasn't holding anything back. He was giving his gifts fully.

And if the man who has nothing dares to give no matter his situation, then we, who have plenty, have no excuses whatsoever.

I will teach you how to give love and be as free as this man. He wasn't waiting for someone to come and help him. He had every reason to see himself as a victim, unable to do anything with his life. He had every reason to spend his life complaining.

But he didn't. He knew he was the one.

I will teach you how to be this free. To discover who you really are. To sing your unique song full out, with utter devotion. And most important, to give your gift. To share your unique ray of light in a world that is starving in darkness.

Our world needs you now more than ever.

I think we can agree that we live in pretty amazing times. We can build big buildings, invent the Internet, send people walking across the moon, launch five hundred channels, and create complex car navigation systems.

Yet we still live in a world where children are starving and millions are homeless.

We have lots of sex but don't make love, bigger bank accounts but less fulfillment, faster cars but no time, more options but less patience, more education but less sense.

More technology, less touch.

Old systems and paradigms are collapsing. We are desperately in need of conscious, awake people who are aware of the power they have within them to re-create the world. Who understand why we are here on this planet. Who are ready to step up and give their gifts.

You have been born at this time for a reason. But until we stop looking outside of ourselves for answers, we will continue to watch the world fall apart.

You. Are. The. One.

Throughout this book, I will be referencing whom I consider the great ones. Gandhi, Jesus, Mother Teresa, the Buddha, Martin Luther King, Jr.

Now, were they great because they fulfilled our societal expectations of success? No. For them, it wasn't about fame or money.

They were great because of who they were and how they loved.

If they had been focused on material success, they would never have been doing what they were doing.

But they knew there was a bigger game in town.

The real riches aren't what you possess. The real riches are who you become.

You too can be a great one. We are all great ones. We just have to stop playing so small.

Right now you need to ask yourself: Is the life you are living the life you are *meant* to be living?

If not, it's not too late. It's never too late.

It's time to stop settling.

Dare to play big.

Live like Mozart composed, like Miles Davis jazzed, or like Michael Jordan jumped.

What would happen if you lived like that? Full out, nothing in reserve?

What would your life look like if you lived and loved like Nelson Mandela persevered? Or like Einstein intuited, the Buddha meditated, Picasso painted, Baryshnikov danced, and Pelé played?

Living your life like it was what you were born to do.

Because it is!

It's time to peel away all those survival mechanisms that have been blocking you from being who you truly are.

I will reintroduce you to the fact that You. Are. The. One.

You. Are. The. One.

The world is waiting for you. The *real* you. And being the

real you, the most authentic you, is the greatest gift you can give the world.

You do not need to go anywhere. You do not need to travel to far-off places for inspiration or enlightenment. Right now you can set yourself free. You can be deeply, fully alive.

The fact that you hold this book in your hands means that you are ready.

You.

Are.

Ready.

CHAPTER | 1

DO YOU DARE?

No one else can ever tell you what you truly want.

You are the only one who knows.

Stop following what's expected.

And dare to go after the life you want.

Finding My Own Way

I never had a chance to live a normal life.

For starters, my full name is Ignatius Kutu Acheampong Blackson.

My mother's from Japan and didn't speak a word of anything but Japanese before marrying my father—a Ghanaian healer, who didn't speak a word of Japanese. (He still doesn't.) They wed as strangers, agreeing to marry before they had ever seen each other.

That's what I call blind faith.

I was named after the former president of Ghana, where my father was the spiritual advisor to two presidents and founded more than three hundred churches before the president was murdered and we fled to London when I was three. My first memories are of seeing my father perform amazing miracles. He would literally heal the lame, deaf, and blind. I will never forget being lost in the crowd following my father and watching a crippled woman crawl on the ground, pick up the sand that my father walked on, smear it on her face, and stand up. (I know. I wouldn't have believed it either, except I saw it with my own eyes.)

I grew up seeing proof that miracles happen.

My father founded a church in London, which grew into a collection of West African refugees, Jamaicans, and West Indians. Soon five thousand congregants would gather on Sundays to hear my father preach, to sing songs that reminded them of their homeland, and to pray for healing.

Because I was my parents' only child and male, everyone expected that I would follow in the footsteps of my father and take over his churches one day. This was made clear when I was eight and my father called me up onstage to give a sermon. I had been snoozing in the pews. (I didn't want to be in church, I wanted to be playing soccer with my friends!) I felt a tap on my shoulder and someone said, "Your father wants you to go up and preach."

I sat up, confused, rubbed the sleep from my eyes, and walked up to the podium where my father stood. "Go ahead, son," he said.

I stood in front of the darkened sanctuary, thousands of eyes focused on me, my father looking at me expectantly.

What was I supposed to say?

And then I just began. The words started flowing out of me. Afterward, I didn't even remember what I had said, but the congregation was in tears, deeply moved by the message that had come through me. Evidently I had talked about the power of having a vision, that Jesus, when he needed to feed the crowd of five thousand, didn't look at the meager offerings of a few fish and loaves of bread but instead turned his eyes upward, to the hills. He looked not down at his limitations but up to a higher plane.

After that day, people began calling me "Little Bishop" or "Pastor Kute." And part of me loved it. I loved spirituality. As soon as I could read, I'd curl up in my room with any book I could find. By the time I was thirteen, I had discovered the books on my father's bookshelves and was reading metaphysical tomes by authors like Neville Goddard and Joel Goldsmith. They fed my unquenchable thirst to try and understand life. *Who are we? Where do we come from? Why do we do what we do?* Reading these books helped me to answer some of these questions and to contribute to the many spiritual conversations in our household. My father's attitude has always been "Other than God, what else is there to talk about?"

It was when I read the American self-help gurus of the nineties—Deepak Chopra, Louise Hay, Jack Canfield, and others—that my obsession really took root. These thought leaders weren't limited by having to follow a set of dictates, but were following their own path, away from organized religion, with its churches, collars, and collection plates. They were creating new ways of being spiritual, inside conference rooms and lecture halls.

They were reaching people who had never set foot in a church and inspiring them to lead powerful, meaningful lives.

There was something in their teachings that resonated with me. For my entire life, the power had resided with the preachers and healers, with God. But these teachers believed that the power was within you and me.

And somewhere deep down I began to realize that I wanted to be a part of that kind of spirituality. While I loved my father and knew that he reached hundreds of thousands of people with his preaching and healings, the more I began to read and develop my own belief system, the less I could envision myself staying in London and leading his church. I felt like I wanted to make my own way, develop my own answers, outside of organized religion.

I started sneaking into the empty church late at night to preach to the empty pews. I'd stand there behind my father's podium, staring at the empty chairs in front of me. I'd close my eyes and imagine them filled with people. I'd open my mouth and begin to preach.

In my mind, I wasn't there in the dark sanctuary of my father's church. In my mind I was in Madison Square Garden. I had often watched the World Wrestling Federation matches that took place in that immense stadium. It was the only large venue in America that I knew about.

But exactly where I was preaching wasn't what was important.

What was important was that deep down I felt like something was calling me to America. In London, the only spiritual conversations happening were in churches. There just was nothing like the emergence of spirituality that was happening in Southern California. I had learned a lot from my father and so much from his books, but I wanted to go to America and see if I could find a way to preach, like my father, but to reach a whole different audience and share a whole different message.

I didn't tell anyone how I was feeling. I kept that desire, that dream, buried deep. It felt silly. Crazy. How was I going to get to America? Where would I even go? I didn't know anyone. All I knew was right here in London in this church.

One day shortly after I turned fourteen, my dad made a formal announcement to the church. "My brethren, my son, Kute, will be ordained! He will be taking over my churches!"

The congregation erupted with applause. My father and all who followed him were counting on me to pick up the mantle and lead in his style and tradition, in honor of the old-timers and the new generation alike. They expected me to graduate from high school, go to college, and then come back to my rightful place at the head of the church.

I smiled and nodded at all the applause. But inside, I felt sick to my stomach.

If I was ever going to follow my calling and go to America, I was going to have to tell my father the truth.

So did I walk right up to him after the services and say, *Thanks, Father, for that announcement, but you know, we need to have a chat*?

Yeah, right.

I said nothing. Why? I was afraid.

I was afraid that he would be angry at me for not doing what was expected. I was afraid to listen to the desires brewing deep in my heart.

So I waited some more—another three years, to be exact. I pretended that everything was fine, that I'd take over my father's churches, that nothing was amiss.

What Was I Waiting For?

And then when I was seventeen, I picked up a book about the life of Jiddu Krishnamurti.

Krishnamurti was one of the great spiritual thinkers of our day. And like me, he was expected, at a very young age, to take over a particular spiritual tradition. Krishnamurti and his brother had been adopted by the president of the Theosophical Society, a spiritual organization founded in the late 1800s that moved to India a few years after its formation in New York.

Krishnamurti's adoptive parents soon identified within him the temperament and wisdom that would make him an incredible spiritual teacher. Thus while he was still very young, his parents proclaimed Krishnamurti was the world teacher that the Theosophists had been waiting for. In order to prepare for his impact on the world, they created a new order and made Krishnamurti the head.

And for many years Krishnamurti went along with this plan.

But when he was twenty-nine, Krishnamurti shocked his parents, the Theosophists, and the world by declining this calling, dissolving the order, and returning all the money and property that had been donated to it. He began to teach on his own, unaffiliated, about the power of mankind. "In oneself lies the whole world, and if you know how to look and learn, the door is there and the key is in your hand. Nobody on earth can give you either the key or the door to open, except yourself."

When I read about Krishnamurti's daring choice, I felt like I heard my soul screaming at me and grabbing me by the shoulders, shaking me and shouting, "KUTE! KUTE! Wake up! Stop ignoring me! You too can go your own way. You too can make your own path. Look at Krishnamurti. What would the world be if he'd just followed the path laid out for him?"

From the moment I read those words, I KNEW. I knew.

I had to tell my father.

There was no going back.

The Scariest Moment of My Life

By this time I was about to finish high school, and most of my classmates were preparing to go to college. That's what everyone expected me to do, too. And I could have. I could have put off the conversation for another few years, gone to college, and then faced my father. But after reading Krishnamurti, I didn't want to wait any longer. I didn't want to go to university for four years, learning stuff from an institution, from books, instead of out there, where life was happening. I wanted to go to America NOW, not later. There would always be time for school.

I was tired of waiting. I was ready to start to experience life.

I went to find my mother. My mother is a quiet soul, full of more faith than anyone I know. She has so much trust, in my father, in me, in life. She has always been my biggest cheerleader. My father traveled a lot, so it was often just the two of us at home. We'd developed a very close relationship. I knew I could trust her to help me gather the courage to speak to my father.

I found her in the kitchen, cooking. I walked in and sat at the kitchen table. We'd had countless conversations in this room as I'd work on homework while she was preparing dinner for the two of us. She turned to look at me and smiled.

But today I didn't carry any books with me. My hands were shaking. I tried to press them hard to the table, to calm myself down. But it didn't work. "Mother," I said, "where's Father?"

"He's upstairs resting before evening services," she said as she stirred.

I took a deep breath. "I think I have to tell him something," I said quietly.

She turned to look at me and saw the expression on my face. She put down the spoon, wiped her hands on a towel, and came to sit down next to me. She took my shaking hands into her own tiny ones.

"Yes, Kute, what is it?"

"I'm not going to do it. I can't take over his ministry. I just . . . I want to do something else. I want to go to America and see what kind of life might be waiting for me there," I said, thankful to have gotten it out.

"You want to go to America?" she asked.

I nodded my head.

"After college?" she asked.

I shook my head no.

"Okay," she said quietly, nodding. "Okay. I know you are afraid, but your father will understand. Deep down, Kute, he just wants you to be happy. Do you think this will make you happy?"

I nodded.

"Then I'll do everything I can to help you get to America," she said as she squeezed my hands.

I jumped up from the chair and enveloped her in a hug. "Thank you," I whispered into her hair. It felt so good to get the truth out to the one person I loved so deeply and to have her tell me it was okay. And that she'd help me.

I now faced the harder task.

My mother had supported me at every juncture of my life. I knew that she would support this decision as well. But my father? We had a different relationship. I knew he loved me, but I felt a deep level of expectation from him. The day that he called me onstage to preach when I was eight, he did nothing to prepare me for it; he just expected that I would handle it. And he has expected me to do the right thing ever since.

Up until this moment I had never let him down.

My mother directed me upstairs, where my father was resting in his bedroom. She waited at the foot of the stairs as I continued on. I turned around in terror.

"Go," she whispered.

I took each step slowly. Part of me wanted to stop and turn around and run back to my room. *Forget it. It can wait. Maybe you don't really need to go to America. Give it up.*

But the other part of me—the part that believed that there was something *calling* me to America—was stronger. That part of me forced me to keep walking up the stairs, even though I felt like each foot was a fifty-pound weight, each step heavier than the last.

I finally made it to the landing. I stood in front of his door. I knocked.

"Come in," I heard.

I slowly opened the door. My father was lying on the bed, his eyes closed. When I entered, he opened them and sat up. "Yes, son, what is it?"

"Father," I stammered. "I have to tell you something."

My father turned and placed his feet on the floor. He motioned for me to sit on the bed next to him.

I shook my head no. I just needed to do it.

"I'm not going to take over your churches. I can't . . . It's . . . not what I want to do," I said. I felt like blood was rushing to my head; I could hardly even hear my own voice.

My father nodded slowly. He looked me in the eye. "Are you sure?" he said, his eyes solemn.

"Yes," I said, nodding.

"Are you *sure*?" he asked again.

I nodded.

"Okay, then," he said. And he lay back down.

I was dismissed.

I quickly ran out of the room, down the stairs, past my mother, and out of the house.

I didn't stop running. Tears were streaming down my face. I knew in some ways I'd broken my father's heart. I'd crushed one of his dreams.

But I'd finally made room for my own.

As I ran, the sadness started to melt away.

Instead, I just felt . . . free.

For the first time in my life.

Free Fall

We all face moments in life where we feel that impulse inside to do something different. But we often stay where we are, where it is comfortable, rather than daring to dream big.

It's not worth it.

Safety is not a recipe for success.

But you've got to be prepared for the free fall.

There's a moment after you do something daring when you go, "Oh, shit! What have I done?"

The moment after you jump out of a plane or off a cliff.

The moment you first say "I love you."

The moment you tell someone the truth you've been holding back.

The moment you leave the job you hate to start your own business.

It's a free fall.

You don't know whether to look up for something to grab on to or look down for something to cushion your fall.

In the fear, in the uncertainty, is the invitation of life.

I've learned more than once that the degree to which you embrace the unknown is the degree to which you are free.

That night I lay in bed. Terrified. Exhilarated. But freaking out. As I lay there unable to sleep, on the cusp of what felt like the beginning of my life, I prayed. "God! If you are real, if you are really up there, you have to help me. I want to follow you, but I do not know what I am doing. I do not know how I will ever get to America. Please, please help."

It was probably one of the truest, most humble prayers I have ever uttered.

A few days later, I was in the library of my school, surrounded by all my classmates preparing to leave for college, and there I was, with no college acceptance, no money, and no plan. I had always excelled at school, and yet when others asked what I was doing next year, I didn't have an answer.

And then a man I had never seen before came up and gave me a copy of *The Economist*. He didn't say anything. He just walked up, put the magazine on the table in front of me, and walked away.

Um, thanks, man!

I'd never read *The Economist* before. I looked at the cover. Curious, I started flipping through it until I got to the section in the back where they include a number of advertisements.

And got chills as I read one of them.

> The American Government is giving away 55,000 green cards in the green card lottery. Apply now!

I kid you not.

As I said, I got chills.

And I knew.

That was my message from the universe. *You have support. This will happen.*

I practically ran home that afternoon and showed the ad to my mother. We called the American law firm that was handling the submissions and had them send us the proper forms in the mail. We filled them out carefully and mailed them back. The law firm would then submit them to the government. The winners would be announced by September 18. If you hadn't heard anything by September 18, you hadn't won a visa.

That was the longest summer of my life.

You can imagine how many days I ran out to the mailbox, praying that this would be the day my dream came true.

Day after day, nothing came.

Finally September 18 arrived.

And there was no visa waiting for me in the mailbox.

Well, I'm not going to lie. I was a bit pissed at the universe.

I picked at my dinner that night. My mother tried to assure me that there would be another way. But I was ready to give up. That ad had been an answer to my prayer! How could it not have come through?

Still angry, I went to bed and spent several hours tossing and turning. But then at midnight, BBBRRRRRING!

My mother rushed into my room. "Kute, a lawyer is on the phone for you!"

I bounded out of bed and into my parents' bedroom, where the receiver was sitting on my mother's side of the bed.

I picked up the receiver.

"Is this Mr. Blackson?" an American voice asked.

"Yes, it is," I responded, my palms slick and clammy.

"This is the law firm that applied for your green card on your behalf. I'm calling to tell you we've just received your notification today. You have won a green card!"

"No," I said in shock. Then "Thank you! Thank you! Thank you!" I was jumping up and down, my mother watching with amusement.

The lawyer explained that I would be receiving the visa in the mail in a matter of weeks.

I hung up, shaking from head to toe. This time not out of fear, but out of joy.

It was all worth it. The years I kept the dream buried. The terrifying moment when I told my father what I wanted to do. The many questions I received from my peers when I told them I wasn't going to college.

I was going to America.

La-La Land

Throughout my life, every time I have taken a chance that has seemed crazy at the time, life has come through for me. I believe that your dreams were given to you for a reason. And that encoded in your dreams are the seeds for its fulfillment. But you have to learn to trust life. You have to learn to let go of safety and not to surrender to fear.

You have to dare to dream.

Are you living the life of YOUR dreams? Don't snuff out those feelings of dissatisfaction that you carry inside. Those feelings are there for a reason. They are beckoning you to something bigger. They are asking you to dare to live the life of YOUR choosing.

So when you find yourself saying, "Well, I'm happy enough. This is good enough," let me tell you something: Life is not about compromise.

Do not compromise whatever dream may be bubbling in your heart.

That impulse to dream, to dare, to discover . . . comes from your soul.

We've been taught to live small. We've been taught to seek a nice, comfy life with a big house and a family and a job that pays the bills. That's what we are supposed to want. That is supposed to be good enough. That's what "normal" people want.

But it doesn't always fill you up, does it?

Here's what I have to say.

To hell with normal.

It's not all it's cracked up to be.

Is normal staying in a relationship with someone you don't love because that's what your family expects of you?

Is normal to have a job you hate just to pay the bills and to keep up with those around you?

Is normal abusing your body with all sorts of artificial drugs and medical procedures to fit what the media deems as beautiful?

Is normal postponing happiness until you retire?

Trying to be normal is a recipe for mediocrity.

You were not made for a normal life.

Because normal denies you the chance to be yourself.

It ignores the unique, beautiful mark you can leave on the world. As unique as your fingerprint. As stunning as the most magical sunset.

To be normal you've got to try and fit in.

While the world is starved for your unique ray of light.

So shed the layer. You are not normal.

Stop pretending you're a lightbulb when you are really the sun.

Nothing great was done by fitting in and being normal and walking the path that everyone walks.

Gandhi. Picasso. Bob Marley. John Lennon. Maya Angelou. Richard Branson. Martin Luther King, Jr. J. K. Rowling. Nelson Mandela. Elvis Presley. Muhammad Ali. Elon Musk. Bruce Lee. Oprah. Malala Yousafzai.

These people are great because they dared to question the status quo.

The moment you leave status quo in the dust is the point at which you can see your life unfold bigger and better than ever before.

When I won my green card, I decided I'd move to Los Angeles. The epicenter of the American spirituality movement was in Southern California, and I knew I wouldn't be the only crazy one in LA, arriving with just a suitcase and a dream. LA was the place for dreamers. I'd fit right in.

I didn't know anyone there. I didn't know where I was going to stay. But I had bought a map of Los Angeles and had studied it every night. All the roads, the neighborhoods. Street by street, I committed it to memory.

My mother helped me buy a plane ticket to LA and then gave me $1,200. Now, we did not have much as a family. Everything was shared with the church. We didn't even own the house we lived in; it was owned by the church. I have no idea how my mother managed to accumulate this kind of cash. But she knew I needed something to get me started. I'd need a place to live, money for food. She wasn't going to be there to take care of me. I'd be on my own.

It was an amazing gift she gave me.

The morning of my flight, I woke up calm. Something about this felt destined, as if it was bigger than me. I ate one last breakfast with my parents and then grabbed my two suitcases. One was filled with clothes, the other with my beloved books. As I said goodbye to my mother, she kissed me on the cheek and said, "I love you. Call me when you get there."

And then she sent me on my way.

My father and I got in the car. We drove the hour and a half to the airport in silence. He parked the car and helped me check my two bags. When we got to the security lines, it was time to say goodbye.

I turned toward him. He smiled and laid his hand on my forehead. He gave me a blessing. "My son, you have a mission in your life. I bless your soul. I bless your journey. I bless you. I love you."

I hugged him and then turned toward security. I wove through the lines and then looked back at my father. He raised his hand in goodbye. And then turned away and walked toward the exit.

I couldn't see him anymore.

I was on my own. And I was exactly where I was meant to be.

I often say that the day I told my father I would not be taking over his churches was the day I became a man.

It was the day I took responsibility for my life. It was the day when I finally acknowledged how I was feeling, finally listened to the cry of my soul.

What if I hadn't allowed that voice to emerge?

I'd probably be preaching in my father's church today.

Is that a bad thing?

No.

But was it what I really wanted to do?

No.

I might have looked successful on the outside.

But I know, I know, that inside, my soul would be dying.

Don't be afraid of your dreams.

Your dreams have chosen you for a reason. Because you are the perfect person to fulfill them.

Yes, YOU.

You just have to say yes. And then the universe will respond.

If you dare to look inside and discover what you truly want, like really deeply want—more than money, more than sex, more than the Cubs winning the World Series—find it, and dare to make it happen? The universe will find a way.

I am living proof.

Playing small serves no one. When you shine your light, it reminds those around you of the very same light inside themselves. You being yourself fully is the greatest gift you can give the world.

CHAPTER | 2

JUST WHO DO YOU THINK YOU ARE?

When we were young, we believed deeply that anything was possible. We had big dreams. Be a baseball player, be a fireman, be a princess, go to the moon.

But along the way, people teach us to be realistic. Not to dream so big. You don't want to be disappointed, do you?

So we get disconnected from our dreams. We get disconnected from our soul.

We get disconnected from who we really are.

I think it's time you got reacquainted with the real you.

Liberate or Bust!

It has been a long journey from the moment I stepped onto American soil with nothing to where I am today. It's been a journey filled with miracles, and I'll tell you all about them throughout this book. Slowly but surely I began to get connected with the very people I'd dreamed about meeting. Eventually I began to speak in front of people. I got a radio show. I started to work one-on-one with clients.

It was far from easy. I had moments of extreme despair, days spent in my tiny studio apartment crying, praying, and trying to figure out what the heck I was doing and who I really was.

Even if we work really hard trying to make something happen in our lives, if we don't know who we truly are and what we truly want, we can have everything in the world and still not be truly happy.

After five years in LA, I was still stuck in many ways. Stuck trying to make things happen, struggling to be in control. Stuck in ego-driven desires. And I needed to do something drastic to break myself out of the pattern I was in.

I was trying to preach freedom, yet I knew I was far from free.

So I packed my bags and began to travel.

One of the first places I traveled was India.

I had always dreamed of visiting India. In the books I read as a boy, India was described as a place teeming with life and light, a far cry from the dark streets of South London. It was a place saturated with the duality of life, the sacred and the profane, the most beautiful temples and the most devastating slums.

The real India did not disappoint.

As soon as I, a wide-eyed, excited, exhausted twenty-three-year-old, stepped off the plane, the sights and smells just hit me. People were . . . everywhere. They rode in cars, in buses packed with passengers, and on mopeds, overflowing with three or four people hanging on. People spilled out onto the street during the day and walked barefoot through the trash that littered every surface; they slept out on the sidewalks at night.

At first I felt overwhelmed with the intensity, the crowds, the nonstop honking of horns, and the sight of people living with next to nothing. Though I wasn't as sheltered as the Buddha, I imagine that my emotions were similar to what the Buddha experienced when he left his palace. Utter shock and deep sadness at how all of this had been going on . . . and I didn't even know.

But as you'll find out in these pages, India is a magical place. And her magic soon began to work on me. From the moment I first set foot on her soil, I realized that India slaps you out of your sleepwalking. It's like BAM! She smacks you upside the head and you can't help but walk away transformed.

A few weeks into my trip, I was in Bihar, the poorest state in India, trying to catch a train out of town. I was running late, and the train was pulling away from the station just as I arrived. I ran like hell and managed to jump onto the last car—which was the third-class section of the train.

Standing in the doorway, I stared at the scene in front of me.

I had no way to prepare for this.

There were no seats. The people were packed in like sardines. The sights, the colors, and the smells were unbelievable. Other passengers stared at me, wondering what was wrong with this man blocking the doorway of the train, the only place where fresh air could filter into the packed car. But I couldn't move.

While I had already been confronted with poverty in India, here, I realized, I would be sitting with the poorest people in the world.

For hours.

I found a small section of floor on which to sit.

We were shoulder to shoulder. I could smell and taste their sweat. I could feel the heat from their bodies. I could feel their hearts. I could feel their suffering.

I could feel their pain. In a way I had never truly experienced before.

I looked around at the people beside me. I knew they had nothing. No food, literally no place to lay their head. All I could think of was the comforts I had back in LA. My apartment, my car, pillows, food in my refrigerator. When I was living my life there, I didn't think of the rest of the world. I didn't think of these people who were struggling to survive.

I took some deep breaths. As I sat there, I noticed a mother with five children sitting just in front of me. Her children were sprawled across the floor. Some of the kids were sick, throwing up, and the vomit was rolling onto my feet. I wanted to recoil. I wanted to escape it. But there was nowhere to go. There was nothing to do. I just had to sit there in the vomit, among all this suffering.

Then something made me look up. And my eyes met those of the mother in front of me.

She stared back at me.

And in her eyes I saw myself. And I felt that she saw herself in my eyes. She knew it and I knew it. In fact, we smiled at each other. It was not a huge grin. It was a small, tired, tearful smile. A smile of recognition. A smile of connection.

A smile that acknowledged we were in two different bodies. But we were one.

An indescribable feeling of love came over me. I felt filled to the brim with love for each and every person on that train in India. In the world.

After several hours, smelling of sweat and vomit, I got off the train—freer than I've ever been. I began running down the street screaming, "I love you! I love you! I love you!" to everyone I saw. I can imagine that people must have thought that I had lost my mind. And in a sense I *had* lost my mind and found something much bigger. I felt as though I had found myself, my true self, which was part of every living and breathing thing in the universe. That was freedom. Right there, in that train in India, I felt free. And from that moment on, I knew that if I could help people realize that deep within them was a soul that was powerful and beautiful and infinite, we could all access that sense of freedom I had just experienced.

This was the moment when I started to think about bringing clients to India. As I sat there staring at that woman, in the mess of life, I began to wonder. What if the president had been here, experiencing this? Would he lead differently? What if Oprah had been here, experiencing this? What would she go back and do? What if the heads of industries and governments were here? Would they be able to run their countries and companies the same way? Would it take them deeper inside themselves so that they saw the interconnectedness of all humanity?

I knew it wouldn't be a journey for everyone. People would have to truly be called to this experience. I would have to feel it and they would have to feel it. But I knew that for those who had gotten stuck in their lives, going to India could completely unravel them so they could finally be free.

So that's what I did. When I got back to LA, I began to determine if certain clients might be ready for the Liberation Experience. It wasn't something to sign up for on a whim. You had to feel called to it, and I had to feel the call as well. But I've now taken almost twenty people. And it is a powerful experience.

At the airport, I take away my clients' passports. Their money. Their cell phones. Their computers. They are left with nothing but a backpack, a single change of clothes, and a journal. There is no communication with family members. They aren't in charge of one single thing on the journey. They leave everything to me. They do not know where we are going or what we are doing.

It is an exercise in trust. I am asking:

Do you trust me? Do you trust life?

Usually the answer is no.

This inability to trust life is a key to their suffering. But on this trip they *have* to trust me.

On the plane ride over, I give clients an assignment.

For the entire twenty-four-hour journey, I ask them to write their autobiography.

I don't let them sleep. I make them keep writing. Page after page after page. Childhood, school, college, career, love stories, children, failures, successes, deaths, and births.

It is exhaustive. And exhausting.

But through the process they are able to access buried memories. They discover recurring patterns. They realize the identities they have been clinging to that have been getting in the way of their true nature.

Because as soon as we get to India, it's like BAM!

You begin to question . . . everything.

It starts as soon as we land. Remember, it's a long journey from the United States to India—sometimes taking more than two days—and once we finally arrive, my clients usually look at me tiredly. My clients have come to India for the promise of transformation, but at this moment they just want to close their eyes for a bit. Maybe find a shower. Those are the things they think they need.

It isn't what I give them.

Oh, sure, we eventually find a hotel room to set down our stuff and get some shut-eye. But this trip is about breaking them free of what they THINK they need. Breaking them free from who they THINK they are.

I push them to their limit.

I make them face the unfaceable.

Anything that might make the client say, "Oh no, I could never do that."

Really, you think you can't do that?

Yes, you can.

Run ten miles?

Yes, you can.

Speak in front of hundreds of people?

Yes, you can.

Fast for twenty-four hours?

Yes, you can.

Face your death?

Yes. You. Can.

Yeah, it's pretty intense.

It's not just about their physical limits. It's about the mental limits, their fears and insecurities and the ways they've been trapped. It is an inner and outer journey. They have agreed to take this radical leap because, despite all they've attained in the world, they know something vital is missing.

It's their connection to themselves. To their soul. To the power that dwells deep within when they dare to access it.

But to access it they've got to peel away the BS ideas they have about who they are.

It's a powerful moment to realize:

What if who you are is not who you *think* you are?

Just Who Do You Think You Are?

It's not like you have *never* known who you are. In fact, the moment you were born, you were just a little soul in a tiny body. When you were born, you were whole, perfect, and complete. No one expected anything of you. You were fully in touch with your divinity. There was no need for yoga. You didn't make time to pray and meditate.

You just WERE.

As a child, you didn't need to find yourself. You hadn't LOST yourself! You were in touch with your soul. You were connected to your *essence*. You were completely free! You danced on the table naked and sang at the top of your lungs. You wore purple polka dots with red stripes and felt fabulous. You examined a blade of grass as if it contained the entire universe. *Because it does.*

You were free. Free of self-consciousness. Not afraid of rejection. In touch with being alive.

But the longer we live in the world, the more we get conditioned to second-guess our natural impulses, the more we begin to squelch our feelings, and the more we begin to question whether who we are at our core is really enough to get the love we are so desperate for.

It starts small. We did something that embarrassed our parents. *Be quiet.* CLICK.

We came home with bad grades and learned that trying hard wasn't good enough. *You need to work harder.* CLICK.

We learned that being LOUD and excited wasn't acceptable. *You need to calm down.* CLICK.

Behave.
Be polite.
Play it safe.
Do the right thing.
Don't be weird.
Be normal.

From the moment we can talk, we face these messages from all sides. Our parents, our teachers, TV, advertisements, the Internet.

And BOOM! Our spontaneity is squashed. We learn to shut down our impulses.

We start to diminish ourselves.

As a coping mechanism, we grow up, ultimately deciding that we have to be someone we're not in order to fit in, in order to be accepted, in order to survive.

We start to ask, *Who do I need to be in order to be loved?*

You see the difference?

We learn to ask not *Who am I?* But

Who do I need to be?

That's the moment. That's the moment we cut the ties with our soul and start to live a lie.

Who we need to become is different for each of us. It depends on our family dynamic. How our parents treat us. What gets us the attention we so desperately seek.

Well, Dad pats me on the head when I'm nice. Oh, okay, ***I'm the nice guy.*** I get validated and accepted this way. That's what I'll keep doing.

Or, *Wow, Mom took me out for ice cream when I brought home good grades. I want to do that again.* ***I'm the smart one.*** I'll just keep getting good grades and achieving more to keep that look of pride on her face.

Or, *Okay, when we don't have money, Mom and Dad fight. So the answer to happiness must be more money. I'm never going to be without money again. I'm going to do everything I can to make it big so I never have to worry.* ***I'm the successful one.*** Look at all I've accomplished!

Day by day, experience by experience, we discover what persona gets us the attention we're so desperate for. And in the process we get molded into people WHO WE ARE NOT. This creates a pattern, a way of being that we call "ME." And this limited expression becomes the whole of our personality.

But we are so much more.

So who have *you* learned to be?

It's time to shed the persona so you can discover the real you buried underneath.

Letting Out the Lion

One of the first clients I took to India was Clark, a good-looking gentleman in his midfifties. He was married to a very successful woman, and despite running his own profitable business, he seemed to live in her shadow. She was the one driving their lives and Clark would meekly follow along.

Now, I had been working with Clark's wife for years, and I was shocked when Clark said he wanted to do the Liberation Experience. He'd always seemed a bit skeptical about me, so when I got his phone call I didn't know what to think. So I suggested we set up a meeting.

As soon as Clark walked into my office, I knew. I knew he had to come to India. Because I could tell that the shy, quiet, timid man was just a persona. I could feel the power within him that was being completely suppressed.

I looked at him and the very first words I said were:

"You're a lion who's been living like a mouse."

Clark stared at me in the doorway. He hadn't even sat down and I had just cut him to the core. And I was right: He wanted to go to India not because he was deeply unhappy with his life, but because both he and his wife could tell that he was living half of a life. He was holding back, in his career and with his wife and his kids.

There was something keeping him stuck. So a few months later, we headed to India.

On the journey over, Clark focused on writing his life story. We didn't speak much during our travels, but during a layover in Hong Kong I asked him some questions about his childhood. He was evasive and shifted uncomfortably as soon as the subject of his childhood came up.

Okay, I thought to myself. *We've got a long way to go.* And I wasn't just talking about the flight.

Finally we landed in India. I asked the cabdriver to drop us off at the steps of the Haji Ali mosque in Mumbai. Our hotel was right around the corner, but it was the middle of the night, and I wanted Clark to experience the calm before the dawn.

"Enjoy this peace while she sleeps through the night, because as soon as the sun rises, India will come to life," I said to Clark as we set our backpacks down and sat on the steps. We would check into our hotel soon. But I could sense something was going on with Clark.

Clark was quiet. I could tell that he was physically and emotionally spent from the travel and his writing assignment. He looked at me, his eyes welling up with tears. "Kute, I cried for the last four hours of our flight here," he confessed. He wiped his nose and continued.

"I don't know why I hadn't remembered this, but somehow, when I was writing on our way here, on the flight from Hong Kong, I remembered something that . . . that I haven't remembered for forty years. Kute, I haven't told *anyone* this. Not my parents, not my wife, not my best friend. No one." He paused and closed his eyes. He took a deep breath.

He opened his eyes. "When I was five," he said quietly, "I was molested by my uncle."

As soon as the words came out, he began to sob. His shoulders were heaving, tears were streaming down his face, and out of his body came the sounds of deep, deep grief. The kind of crying you do when you've gotten the phone call you've always dreaded. The kind of wailing for when someone you love has died.

And he was mourning. He was mourning the fact that as a five-year-old boy, he had covered up this scary, horrifying act that stole all innocence from him.

I sat next to Clark and laid my hand on his shoulder. Tears began to stream down my face as well. I knew that accessing this memory was the first step of many to set him free.

I didn't want to push too hard. I wanted to let him feel this grief. There was nothing else to do but cry in that moment.

But this was huge for Clark. And it explained so much of his behavior as an adult.

Bring It to Light

What stories are you hiding?

As young children, we learn to avoid uncomfortable emotions. To pretend that everything is okay. We have been conditioned to suppress pain. Remember all those moments when our parents tried to soothe us by saying, "Don't cry, it's okay"? This tells us that such emotions aren't okay, that we should shove them under the rug.

But when Clark was finally given the space to write about his life, to step out of the small box of the life he had created for himself—when he was going into a foreign land, a place unfamiliar to him, where all the things he depended on to keep him safe were gone—this memory had room to resurface. It had been there all along, waiting to come out, waiting for his carefully constructed survival mechanisms to shift so he had some room to finally breathe. It was only when he discovered the truth that he could see why he was living such a small life.

Think of it this way: When you were born, you were like a huge, crisp white sheet of paper. You were smooth. You were expansive. You were full of possibility.

And then life happens. You were told to stop crying. And part of you crumpled up. You were bullied in school. Crumple. Your parents divorced. Crumple.

Before too long, you look nothing like that pristine sheet of paper. You are just a crumpled-up little ball.

Where you once felt like spreading your arms and shouting to the world THIS IS ME!

Now you cower in the corner in your little ball and whisper, *This is me.*

When Clark was molested, he began to believe that it would be safer for him to hide in his life. So he hid the truth of what happened. And he began to put on the persona of the quiet one. The shy one. The nice guy. They were personas that he had erected to keep him safe.

If you didn't know he was there, if he didn't attract any attention—you couldn't hurt him.

Because he had stifled this memory, he didn't realize that it was truly CONTROLLING HIS LIFE.

Now, fifty years later, he was trapped in that shy guy persona. There was a reason his wife felt frustrated by his inability to truly communicate. He was living in that limited persona. When you think you are the nice guy, it means you can't get at the part of you that dares to make people uncomfortable; you can't ask for what you need. When you are the shy one, it means you can't risk speaking the truth or telling people how you really feel.

When we try to squeeze ourselves into a persona, we suppress all the parts of ourselves that don't fit into that character.

To be the good boy, you've got to suppress your anger. To be the funny one, you've got to quiet the smart and serious side of you. To be the angry girl, you've got to squash down your joy. You've got to continue to find things to be angry about.

That's why it was so hard for me to tell my father the truth. I'd been raised to be the good boy, the obedient son. In order to tell my father the truth, I had to break out of my persona. It took three years for me to gather the courage to do so. Essentially, I waited as long as I could. Until I faced a fork in the road. Go to the university and do what is expected? Stay in that persona? Or try something new?

What aspects have you suppressed your entire life? Your sexuality? Your creativity? Your anger? Your sadness?

In the process of holding on to your persona, you suppress the naturalness of your being. You spend so much energy trying to be proper, keep it together, fit in, look good, be liked, be appropriate, and not say the wrong thing that you end up feeling as if you are holding your breath. You don't want to move. It's like when you need to yawn but feel as if you shouldn't yawn. So you go through life holding back. Holding back the natural impulse to be WHO YOU TRULY ARE!

To be truly powerful requires that you get in touch with the entire range of yourself. All aspects of yourself. All shades of the rainbow of your being, not just a few colors.

Whether you've gone through life as the shy one, the life of the party, the damsel in distress, or the drama queen, recognize that there is more to who you are. Those personas are just patterns of conditioning that you learned to follow in order to survive. The strategy may have worked for you when you were five or ten or fifteen, when you lived in the shadow of your parents and were desperate for acceptance and love.

But now you are an adult.

Take a look at what persona you think has been "working" for you all these years.

It is NOT who you are.

And it hasn't really been working, has it?

Stepping Out

Soon after Clark's revelation, we checked into our hotel. We got some sleep. And then we headed to the train station. Clark's realization was key to his freedom, but we had only just scratched the surface. There was still a lot of work to do in India.

Clark looked excited. Where were we headed to next?

But I told him to sit down on platform one.

"Clark, we are going to sit here. That's all we are going to do. We are going to sit. I want you to just watch what is going on around you. The people coming and going. The children coming up and begging. We're just going to sit."

For the first hour Clark looked around, his eyes shining brightly. This was our first day in India, and he was excited the journey was beginning.

After several hours he asked to use the restroom.

I pointed to where the bathrooms were located in the corner of the station.

I watched him walk over to them and talk to one of the guards positioned outside.

He soon turned around and came right back, sitting down next to me.

"What happened?" I asked.

"You have to pay," he said, resigned.

"Okay, well, would you like some money to go to the bathroom, Clark?" I said with a smile.

He nodded silently.

"Well, why didn't you just ask?" I said.

He shrugged his shoulders.

This was such a picture of Clark's life. He was always a follower, not wanting to disturb anyone, so he kept quiet and didn't ask any questions. This was why he was so cut off from his power.

When he came back from the restroom and sat down next

to me again, I knew I had to show him how futile this persona was.

"Listen, Clark, it's time to move out of this pattern. As a kid, you were so bright; you shone so innocently, tenderly, vulnerably. Then someone saw that light and took advantage of you. On an unconscious level you are still choosing to hide so that no one can see you. You think that you can avoid pain and hurt if you live in the safe zone, living in your wife's shadow. But is that really enough for you?"

Clark shook his head.

"Okay, Clark, let's say you got into a car accident and you woke up in a hospital bed with no memory of who you were and why you were in a hospital. Wouldn't you stare down at your body in confusion, asking, 'Who am I?' "

Clark looked at me. "I don't know. That would be terrifying."

"Say the doctor walks into the room and says your memory loss is permanent. He says your name is Sam, you have a beautiful wife named Jessica, and you live in a nice house in Vancouver. You are a banker and have a very successful business. You have three kids. Isn't it time you went back to them? And then he puts you on a plane and you go to Vancouver to live with Jessica and the three kids. What happened to Clark? Who is he?"

Clark shook his head. "I don't know. I guess he wouldn't really exist anymore."

"Exactly. All the things you think define you are just part of a story that you've been a part of, a story that other people wrote for you. The only thing you would be able to know for sure in that hospital room is 'I am. I am alive.' Everything else is just a part of a story, a script, and you are so much more than that story.

"You think you are the shy one, the quiet one, the nice guy. But you are so much more. Everything you put behind the words 'I am' is a concept that someone else must tell you. *Husband, father, brother, sister, employee, Harvard MBA, boss, mother, lover, artist, banker, cabdriver, entrepreneur.* Those are just roles. They don't really tell you anything about who YOU are. Because can your job, your degree, your roles really define *you*?"

He shook his head.

"Look, Clark, here we are on platform one. We've been sitting here all day. Platform one. Imagine, Clark, that you lived on platform one. This was your entire life and you never left this platform. This was all you knew. Well, there's a whole wide world out there beyond the bridge. You can live on platform one the rest of your life, meaning you can live in the limited identities that you've gotten comfortable with, or you can break free."

At this point I got up from where we were sitting and began to dance awkwardly, my hands moving in a rhythmic robotic pattern. "It's time to step out and shake up your dance. No matter what music life is playing, there you are, Clark, doing a five-step dance. It's tiring and limiting. It doesn't go with the music. You use the same dance moves for everything. Or think of it this way: When you build a house, do you use the same tools for everything? If I used a screwdriver for every single thing that was necessary, you'd look at me like I was crazy! So why do you do that with your life?"

Clark nodded. He was beginning to see what his persona was costing him.

"What if you broke out and started to freestyle?"

I stopped dancing, an idea now percolating in my heart.

"C'mon, Clark, you are coming with me."

We exited the station and wandered through the streets until we found what I was looking for. A group of men sitting on a street corner, listening to music and playing drums.

"Now, Clark," I said, "I want you to dance like your persona. I want you to do the dance of the nice guy, the shy and quiet one, the follower. What does that look like?"

He began to kind of bob his head to the music. His movements were small, contained, and awkward. It looked as if he didn't want anyone to notice him. As if he didn't want anyone to even see him.

I let him feel the awkwardness of his dance.

"You know that you are more than that, right? What would you dance like if you were able to access your soul? What would you dance like if you could be that carefree five-year-old again? What would you dance like if you knew that at any moment you could choose a new move?"

Clark began to move more aggressively to the music. He began to move his hips and wave his arms. Now there was a crowd gathering to watch and people began to dance with him, following his moves, encouraging him.

"Okay, Clark, now I want to you to dance with your eyes closed. Close your eyes and just feel the music. And let your body follow!"

Sweat was pouring down his face. There was a moment when I could feel him cross over. It was as if he physically stepped out of the prison of his persona. He broke out of his five-step dance. And his spirit began to improvise. He wasn't thinking. He wasn't there. Clark wasn't doing the dancing. It was happening through him. Clark closed his eyes and began to twirl around, moving and shaking like there was nobody watching, nobody judging. Like he was a young boy. And totally free.

"There, Clark! There! That, my man, is who you really are!"

There were probably forty people on the corner with us, bopping to the music, drumming their drums, moving in total freedom and joy.

We all have access to that freedom.

Do you dare to set that persona aside and dance the dance of a free soul?

What are your five steps?

Are you:

the victim
the saint
the drama queen
the martyr

the know-it-all
the rebel

To start to break the grip of your conditioning is to be *aware* of your conditioning. The more you can be conscious and aware of your personas, the less you have to be run by them. Because just like Clark, when you live within a persona, you no longer have range in how you respond to life. There is no creativity, no exploration. There is just a set way of being. And even when the music changes, you still have just five dance moves. Reggae? Mozart? Hip-hop? Jazz? It doesn't matter. You've got only five steps.

Listen, we don't always get to choose the music that gets played in our lives. It's not always going to be Mozart; it's not always going to be beautiful. But if you are stuck in five steps, you are always doing the same dance. You look pretty awkward with your hip-hop moves when the music being played is salsa. The freer you are, the more you are able to spontaneously meet the moment with right action. But when you are trapped in your persona, you can only sway awkwardly to the music, feeling confined, like you are out of sync, but you don't have any other options. You are unable to improvise.

Why do you think people go out and drink to have a good time? Because it allows them to loosen the ties of their persona for a brief moment. To get a taste of freedom. Yet it doesn't last. The moment is fleeting. So they have to go out and drink again and again and again.

But when you shed your persona, you realize that there are infinite possibilities for improvisation. There is SO MUCH MORE TO WHO YOU ARE. There is so much more TO LIFE ITSELF.

What have you been suppressing? What part of you is screaming to be expressed?

The real you is calling.

Free Ride

As Clark and I spent more and more time together, as India continued to unravel him, it became clear that there was a side of him that had been suppressed for fifty years. Deep down, Clark was a bit of a daredevil. Or maybe even a badass! But he'd been suppressing it all these years in his need to conform to his persona. One day at lunch, he confessed that he'd always dreamed of owning a motorcycle and even getting a tattoo. I had to laugh. If his wife knew that deep down Clark wanted to get a tattoo, I knew she would be shocked! This was so different from the man she had access to. The fact that he could even admit this meant he was shedding the layer.

The next morning, we were out running when we saw a motorcycle parked on the side of the road. And emblazoned on the side was the name of the motorcycle: FREEDOM.

I kid you not.

Clark and I both laughed at the gift the universe had sent.

We found the owner of the motorcycle and asked if we

could take a picture of it. Then I asked him if he would take Clark for a ride.

Clark's eyes lit up. And he and his new friend Vinod went riding off through the wild streets of India on a Freedom ride.

Clark came back with his gray hair disheveled, his face dirty, and his eyes on fire.

He was feeling the beating of his soul.

Within each of us is so much possibility. Why do you limit yourself? What would it mean if you would allow yourself to be both the nice guy and the badass, the good girl and the seductress, the bad girl and the good girl? Because it's not about the persona. It's about your relationship with the persona. When your persona owns you, you have no ability to choose.

But when you shed it, when you realize that deep within, you are so much more, then you can be all things. Freedom is about having access to the full range of your expression, not just one or two colors. It doesn't mean that you will never be nice or quiet when you shed that persona. You still have access to that shade, but it isn't your only color.

Underlying each of our personas is a positive intention. Our personas are trying to get us something we desire—love, attention, recognition, happiness. But we are going about it in a limiting way, a way that we learned early in our lives. When we realize that underlying our personas is a positive intention, then we can feel compassion for ourselves rather than judgment.

When I saw Clark getting off the back of the motorcycle,

finally having accessed a part of his soul that he had been suppressing for years, I knew it was time for an initiation.

I decided it was time to make the transformation complete.

As soon as we stepped into the tattoo parlor, Clark was ready. He didn't resist this at all. He knew it was the next step on his journey.

He sat in the chair and I said, "Close your eyes, and as you sit in the chair, feel yourself letting go of the old you. From this moment on, you will have this tattoo. This tattoo represents your initiation into a new phase. You are letting go of your nice guy bit. Your follower personality. Being the quiet, shy one. We're going to let it go. We're going to start over so you can begin to act from a space of freedom. So you can begin to choose in each moment who you are. Do you want to follow? Okay, that's fine, but you are choosing it. Do you want to lead? You are free to choose. You are no longer being run by a persona, by the script of the shy one. See who emerges as you walk on in life. You can be anyone you want to be, Clark. You can be anyone you want to be."

When Clark stepped out of the shop, his chest emblazoned with a soaring eagle, he was transformed. In many ways, before me stood the lion that I knew had been aching to get out.

I often ask myself:

What if he'd never come to India?

What if he'd never accessed that memory?

What if he'd allowed himself to be stuck in that pattern of smallness and shyness and limitedness . . . for his entire life?

So do you dare?

Do you dare to let out the lion?

At any time you can shed the layer.

When you start to feel yourself acting out of your personas, you can make a different choice.

You can check in. *Why am I doing this? Is this what I really want? Is this how I deep down really want to act?*

You can recognize that within you is a whole rainbow of choices.

At the end of the day, who are you trying to win over? Your parents? Your friends? God?

Is it worth it if you sacrifice the power of your soul?

So can you do it? Can you let it go?

The persona, the limits, the five-step dance?

When you rip off the persona, you get one step closer to discovering the power of your soul.

What are you waiting for?

Forget who you **think** ***you are—find out who you*** **really** ***are.***

CHAPTER | 3

UNFINISHED BUSINESS

You hold the lock and you hold the key.

When you take responsibility, you set yourself free.

Own the power you have to create your life. That power is in you. But we've often gotten stuck in patterns that keep us powerless.

In order to move forward in your life, you've got to bring to light the ways your past may be having an impact on your present.

You've got to let the past go. Feel it. Forgive it. Free yourself from it.

Growing Pains

We all have one thing in common.

When you dig down to the root of your conditioning, you will find . . . your parents.

Our parents set our navigational systems.

When we are young, our parents are the ones who make

the rules. They are the ones who determine what classes you take, who your friends are, how you dress, what to believe, what's right and wrong, even what you want to be when you grow up.

They were the first to hold you. The people you spent the most time around. The ones who trained you. Fed you. Taught you how to talk and walk, how to read and swim. What to believe about life, sex, money, relationships. What love is supposed to feel like.

Our personalities developed in reaction to how they treated us. We took on their stories. We took on their patterns. We learned to emulate them in an effort to gain love.

Because of this, many times, even when we become adults, our parents are the constant voices in our head.

Don't do that. What would people think?

Don't date her. She's not wife material.

Keep trying. You're not good enough.

Maybe you think that is *your* voice in your head. But if you start to dig deep, you'll realize it is probably the voice of one of your parents.

They may still be running the show.

Now, look, I love my parents. This is not about parent bashing. Some parents are great and loving. Some are neglectful or overbearing. We don't control what we get. But we've got to admit that we might still be holding on to some unresolved feelings about our parents. Often we don't realize we are holding on to these. It took me years before I could acknowledge that maybe I had a bit of anger toward my parents. If you'd asked me outright, I would reply, "No, of course not! I love my parents!" It wasn't until I peeled away the layers that I could see . . . Oh, yeah, there *is* some unresolved stuff that I have been holding on to.

We all do it. It's only natural. But now we've got to peel back the layers. You see, we think we are free, that we have free will, but when we are not aware of the impact our parents still have on us, we are being run by our conditioning. To the degree that you are run by your conditioning, you are not free to choose and create your future.

I know how deeply our parents can influence us. When I first moved to LA, I felt as if I was leaving my parents behind. Here I was, doing this daring thing, something they didn't choose for me. Something I chose for myself.

But I had underestimated just how much I was dependent on my parents. Not just for financial support but for emotional support. Encouragement.

My parents had been my lifelines for seventeen years. And without their constant presence, I was surprised by how unsteady I felt.

When I first landed in LA, I rushed off the plane like an eager puppy, ready to see what new bone my owner had gotten for me. I collected my two suitcases, speedily went through customs, and then made my way outside. Once I located the taxi stand, I shook the cabdriver's hand. "Hi, I've just moved here and don't know anyone. Can you take me somewhere to stay for a couple of weeks that will be cheap but safe?"

He looked at me with a smile. "Sure, my man. Get in, get in!"

As we made our way through the city, I stared out the window in awe, at the tall, modern buildings, checking all the street signs against the well-studied map that I had pulled out of my pocket.

Soon we pulled up in front of the Venice Beach Cotel. (It wasn't even a motel. This gives you a hint as to its condition.) I stared up at what would be my new home. *Okay, I can make this work*, I thought.

And then I looked around. Venice Beach. There is no place even remotely like Venice Beach in London. As the cabdriver got my suitcases out of the trunk, I took it all in. It was Sunday morning, and the boardwalk was packed. Skateboarders, girls in bikinis, homeless people, vendors trying to sell goods to the many tourists who came here to see this iconic piece of Americana. The sun glinting off the ocean.

It was like WELCOME TO AMERICA, KUTE!

For a couple of days, I just explored. I wandered the beach, the stores, and the cinemas, amazed. But after the initial haze of newness wore off, it hit me. I had left home. I couldn't just go upstairs and see my mom and dad. I was eighteen years old. I knew NO ONE. I was truly alone for the first time in my life.

I called my mom in tears. She tried to console me. "Kute, this is what you dreamed of. There is a reason you are there. Just stop and look for what your next step may be. Go out, find a newspaper, and find an apartment you can rent. Just make that your goal right now. You don't have to do it all at once."

I thanked her and did as she said. Every morning I'd go out to the steps of the lobby of the Cotel, pick up the paper, and flip through it in search of an apartment I could afford. Every few days, I called my mother. With that regular dose of encouragement, I felt okay again.

Finally, after two weeks of crying, calling my mom, wandering the streets, and searching the newspapers, I found a tiny apartment renting in Koreatown for $250 a month. It felt like an enormous sum of money, but I knew it was probably the best I was going to find. As I prepared to move into my new place, I knew I had to find a way to start making some money. Otherwise I was going to be able to stay in America for only a few months. I would have to go crawling back to Mom and Dad with my tail between my legs.

Not an option. I was going to make this work. There was a reason I had won this green card. I just had to trust that the way would unfold.

The day I moved into that tiny studio apartment, I looked around with pride. This wasn't a temporary hotel room. This was an apartment. My apartment. My new home. I had nothing but a dirty mattress that I had found on the side of the road and the two suitcases I had brought with me from London. But as I sat on that mattress in the middle of my own apartment, I felt like I had everything. Now I was finally creating life on my own terms. Becoming an adult.

For each of us, there comes a point when you must choose to step into your adulthood and finally leave your parents behind. This is a necessary step in order to own your power. This must happen. But for many of us, it takes much longer than we think. Some of us never do it, forever remaining attached to them.

Little did I know that despite the fact I was no longer calling home every day, my parents were still there, hovering over me. Theirs were the voices in my head. Theirs was the approval I was still seeking. For the first five years that I lived in LA, I was unconsciously striving to prove myself to my father. Desperately seeking to reach that moment when I could say, *See? I did it! I didn't make a mistake! Look at what I'm doing on my own! I am now a true success!*

That desire to prove to my father I had done something on my own created a pressure cooker of stress and expectations. Every time I hit an obstacle, I would freak out. My ego could not afford my flying back to London.

Whether we are fifteen or forty—or sixty, for that matter—whether we had the best parents in the world and still speak to them every day or we hated our childhood and couldn't wait to move away, many times our parents are still controlling our actions.

Stop for a moment and take inventory over your life. If you were truly free, would you have made some of the choices that you did in your life? You know what I'm talking about. It's those times when you date someone you know is wrong for you, when you accept a job you don't really want, when you go to a college that doesn't match who you are—all in an effort to gain your parents' approval.

You see, our conditioning is deeply rooted. It is unconscious. And it will be in control until you acknowledge it and say, "No more!"

Every single thing that has ever happened to you gets stored in your nervous system. Your nervous system is your antenna to the world. It filters every bit of information that comes your way and interprets it, creating meaning from it. And depending on how much conditioning has accumulated in your nervous system, it creates your reality out of the experiences of your past. Essentially, you are creating your own reality. But that doesn't mean your version of reality is accurate.

For example, if you grew up with parents who were mean or absent, imprinted in your nervous system is the belief that "Love hurts. Love is abusive." Our parents teach us what love looks like. So if it looks abusive, we will go out and seek relationships that match that definition of love. We seek out relationships that feel familiar to our imprint of what love felt like growing up. So if your parents were belittling, you will find yourself in relationships where your lover talks down to you and treats you poorly. Even though such situations are painful, on some level, they feel like home.

But we do not need to go through life with a misguided sense of the world. We can face the impact our parents may have had on us, and then we can let it go. This is our responsibility.

Being Right Versus Being Free

Several years after creating the Liberation Experience, I decided to set up another transformational experience, but this time, I would take a group of people to Bali. Similar to the India trip, this is a twelve-day immersion experience in which I use Bali as a seminar room without walls. I create a unique process that helps participants shed the layers preventing them from accessing who they truly are. This journey is called Boundless Bliss: The Bali Breakthrough Experience. There is nothing like it in the world.

Bali offers a totally different experience from India. While India smacks you out of your sleepwalking, Bali melts you with her beauty. The unraveling that happens in Bali is tender, versus the quick shattering of India. But at the end of the day, the transformation is just as powerful.

Carolina was a young woman who joined me on my first Boundless Bliss trip. She came on the trip because she knew there was something keeping her stuck. She still lived in her parents' basement, she worked a dead-end job, and she kept finding herself in unfulfilling relationships.

She just couldn't seem to find any degree of success.

Clients in Bali examine their life story much as clients in India do. And as Carolina began to talk about her childhood, she described the way her parents treated her with a lot of anger. She recalled being called worthless, being ignored. She admitted that she never ever felt loved by her parents.

As she talked, I sat there thinking, *Why on earth are you still living with these people?*

I knew there had to be a reason she was still subjecting herself to their abuse.

One morning several days into our trip, we headed into the morning session, all tired from the previous day, which like the other days had been intense. The days often began at seven in the morning and continued late into the night, and we would include physical activities like hiking alongside deep psychological work. It was an exhausting process.

As soon as the session began, Carolina spoke up.

"Kute," she said, "I just don't know how much more I can do. I don't think I'm cut out for this."

"What makes you think that you should quit?" I asked. "I understand that you are stretched to your edge, but that is when you can begin to see how strong you really are."

But Carolina shook her head. "I'm not as strong as other people. I really don't think I can do this."

"Why aren't you as strong as other people, Carolina? I think that's a lie you've been telling yourself. "

I looked at this beautiful young woman in front of me. All I saw was potential. Why was it that all she saw was failure?

“Carolina, what is it that is really holding you back? Stop lying to yourself and allow yourself to access the truth. What is really holding you back?”

She shook her head as she gazed out at the ocean. “I don’t know, Kute. I just don’t know.”

“Carolina,” I said, smiling, “that’s bullshit. You know what it is. What. Is. Really. Holding. You. Back?”

She turned to look at me. I stared into her eyes. I was not going to let her avoid the truth any longer.

And finally her face crumpled. And she stammered out the words.

“I can’t succeed.”

“Why?” I asked.

“Because!” And here she began to get angry. “Because then it would make it okay! It would make the way my parents treated me okay. It would mean that it didn’t matter that they didn’t love me, that they ignored me, that they called me names. I can’t do anything with my life, because if I do, they will think they were good parents.” She paused as she began to sob. Finally she whispered, “If I’m a screw-up, then my parents will know that it is all their fault!”

Boom! There it was.

The truth. The payoff.

Often there are things we get out of staying stuck that we aren’t even aware of. But there is always a reason you are still stuck.

"Carolina, that may be true, they may have screwed you up. But the only person that you are hurting right now is you."

Her tears continued to fall.

"Carolina, I have a question for you."

I paused.

"Carolina, do you want to be right? Or do you want to be free?"

She looked at me. "What do you mean?"

"Well, Carolina, you can prove your parents right and stay stuck in a pattern that isn't serving you. You can let the past determine the rest of your life. Or you can admit that yes, you had a horrible childhood, but now you are an adult, now you are in charge, and you can move beyond the past and forgive. Really, the choice is yours. Do you want to be right or do you want to be free?"

She looked at me with tears in her eyes. It was like a lightbulb had gone off.

"I want to be free," she said quietly. "I am ready to be free."

"Okay," I said, "then it is time to let them go."

Power Struggle

I've found through working with thousands of clients from around the world that until we break free from our parents, we are typically reacting in several ways. We are still desperately trying to please them and win their approval—and thus are living lives that aren't truly what *we* want. Or we are rebelling, attempting to make them mad or upset them. Or we are spending our lives trying to prove them wrong.

It doesn't matter which scenario you find yourself in. All three scenarios leave your parents holding the power. What's interesting is that many people think when they are rebelling that they are exercising control. But they aren't. When you rebel, you are still not free. You are "against" your parents, so they are still controlling your attention.

Any way you cut it, they have the power.

The moment you can detach from your parents is the moment you can start to live your own life.

As we sat there in Bali, Carolina looked at me with confusion. "Kute, I don't know how to let them go."

"Don't worry," I said. "I'm going to show you how." I looked at the group around me, who had watched this conversation take place. They had witnessed Carolina holding herself back for the past few days. Everyone was invested in her breaking through. But it wasn't just about Carolina. All of the members of the group had their own issues that they needed to deal with.

"Let's all close our eyes. Now think about your parents. Maybe you didn't have a great relationship and you've always wished for more closeness. Maybe you are like Carolina, and had parents that were abusive. Maybe you had great parents, people who wanted only the best for you, but with that came a lot of expectations that weighed you down and influenced the choices you made in your life."

I paused, letting everyone think.

"What do you want to say to them? I want you to think about what you have been holding back for years. What you've never been able to express. We suppress so much because of our parents. And until we let it out, those subtle unconscious layers of resentment will remain. Now is the time to give yourself permission to let that energy go."

I looked at Carolina. She had spent her entire life trying to avoid her anger at her parents, trying to make it manageable. But it was still driving her life. It was time for her to let it go.

"We all learned to shut down our feelings in order to avoid pain. The pain of your parents fighting. Their neglect. The feeling of not being loved. We suppress our disappointments over not getting a role, not winning a championship, or not getting into a certain college. We think we are protecting ourselves. But when you stuff your emotions inside—anger, fear, sadness, hurt—you can't release them. They just accumulate."

I paused.

"As an adult, you have been stuffing your emotions for so long, you don't even realize you are doing it. It's like when you wear a watch. At first you notice the pressure on your wrist, but ultimately you stop feeling it. It just becomes normal, routine.

"But emotions were created to be felt and expressed, not suppressed."

I took a deep breath. "We are often so afraid of our emotions. Of what might happen if they came out. But there are no good or bad feelings. Feelings are simply energy. We are often taught to believe that certain feelings are better than others. We tend to avoid, deny, disconnect from, suppress, or try to get rid of the feelings that we call 'negative.' But resisting your negative feelings just keeps you stuck. When you stuff all your emotions inside, when you don't allow yourself to process what happens to you, it is like carrying an elephant on your back and trying to run a marathon. You are never going to get anywhere. Now is the time to put that elephant down. To do that, you've got to let those emotions out. Take the labels off and honor the energy you feel moving inside you. Acknowledge the feelings. Experience them. Then move on. When you have an emotion that feels uncomfortable, the key is to embrace it completely. Notice the sensations in your body. Welcome the feeling without judgment. Feelings are simply a signal that you need to pay attention to something within yourself. Something happened that didn't feel good. Those emotions are there for a reason. They want to help you. When you give yourself permission to experience your feelings, they dissolve. When you resist them, they back up and create blockages, preventing you from accessing your soul."

People were nodding their heads; a few already had tears streaming down their faces. They were ready. They were ready to face their parent.

"Okay, I want everyone to stand up. Imagine that standing in front of you is the parent for whom you hold the most unresolved feelings. That parent is there, standing right in front of you. Close your eyes. Feel the presence of that parent. Now, when I stop speaking, it is your turn. I want you to say everything that was never said. All the stuff you held back as a child. All the things you hold back today as an adult. Let it out. No holds barred. Give yourself permission to go for it. Say how you feel. Finally let the truth come to light."

I stopped talking. And in the quiet came a surge of emotion. Everyone burst into tears. Men, women; old, young. They all felt the power of those emotions coming to the surface. And then they began to speak. They began to share all the words they had held back for years. They began to unburden themselves of the suppressed emotions. So that they could finally be free.

The F Word

This is not an easy process. It sometimes takes hours for people to get it all out. To recover from the exhausting emotions, feelings that literally just wear you out. But once people began to quiet down, calm down, and return to their chairs, I knew it was time for the next step.

I turned and looked at the entire group. "Today is the day to stop blaming your parents. Give it up. Stop. Now. Your parents owe you nothing as an adult. They have already given you the greatest gift of all—life itself." I paused to let that sink in.

"They have given you life. Here you are in Bali, breathing

in, breathing out. Looking up at the beautiful sky. Smelling the delicious scent of flowers. All of that is due to their gift. Their gift of life.

"Your parents are what they are. They were what they were before they met you. They are likely to keep being what they are in the future. They owe you nothing anymore. Part of being an adult is taking responsibility for your own life."

Many in the group were nodding. They were ready.

"When we make our parents responsible for what was done long ago, we then don't have to be responsible for what we do today. This is a cop-out, a way to avoid truly living your life. No one else is responsible. Your parents are no longer responsible for the choices you make today. No matter what happened in the past, you have a choice today what you believe and do."

I paused and turned to Carolina.

"Carolina, you get to choose right now. Holding on to anger and resentment is not worth it. Nothing and no one are worth your peace and happiness."

Carolina nodded tearfully.

"Do you believe that? Nothing and no one are worth your peace and happiness. So are you ready?" I asked.

The warm Bali air began to sweep over the bluff, ruffling hair and stirring emotions.

"Now, if you want to be free from your parents, you have to take it to the next level."

I paused.

"The next step is to forgive. When you forgive your parents, you set yourself free. You do not forgive for the other person. You do it for your own freedom. They don't even need to know you have forgiven them. Because . . .

"Forgiveness is something you do for you."

I stood in front of Carolina and spoke to the rest of the students.

"Close your eyes. Whether you were like Carolina, a child desperate for love, or whether you were an adolescent and you disappointed your parents, or whether you just felt a lot of expectations from your parents that you could never live up to, you have a choice to forgive. Forgiveness will not free you until you face, experience, and embrace the feeling that requires forgiveness. Think about the sound of a wave. Coming in and rushing out. Continuous. Listen to that sound. Let that sound dissolve the emotion you are feeling, whether it is sadness or anger or betrayal. We cannot access the power of forgiveness until we first acknowledge the hurt and pain lying beneath the surface. You can say you forgive someone, but unless you have fully felt the betrayal, the hurt, the pain that person caused, it is still there, simmering underneath the surface. To feel is the first step."

People began to shuffle and reposition themselves. Forgiveness is notoriously difficult for all of us. But it is the key to no longer letting the past control your future.

"I want you now to imagine yourself in the body of your parent. You are now your mother or father. Take a deep breath. Access whatever pain they might have been in to hurt you in that way. Feel what they must have felt."

I was silent for a few minutes. As soon as people really felt themselves in the bodies of the people who hurt them, you could see the emotion start to release. This simple process did something powerful. It allowed them to see how the very person that they had been so angry at was human. Was in pain. Was probably just doing the best he or she could in that moment.

"You see, we think it's personal. That it's about us."

I paused.

"It's not about us. It's not about you. When we can begin to feel compassion for the other person, we can begin to forgive. So stop, come back to yourself and who you are today. And in your heart say to that person, 'I forgive you.'"

I paused.

"Now I want you to say it out loud. I forgive you."

I heard a chorus of forgiveness.

"One more time. I forgive you."

This time it was louder.

"Okay, open your eyes."

I looked around at the group as they blinked in the brightness of the Bali sun.

"So I have a question. Are you free?"

The group erupted with a loud YES!

You do not forgive for the other person. You do it for your own freedom.

What unexpressed emotion is running your life?

Stop. Stop. Feel the emotion. It will not kill you. It is just energy. Stop squashing it, trying to snuff it out. Let it burn. And then burn out.

Otherwise the past will run the rest of our lives.

Now is the time to let your parents go.

It's Not About the Relationship Outside

Now, I don't want you to think that letting go of your parents means you are cutting them out of your life. Far from it. It's a wonderful thing to have your parents in your life and honor them—if that feels authentic for you. What I'm talking about is letting go of your need to please your parents or prove them wrong. Letting go of your need for them to be different. They were what they were. You can't change that. Only accept it, to be free.

Sometimes we find it difficult to let go of parents and accept them exactly as they are. Then we will have to admit that we will never have the relationship that we dreamed of. Sometimes we refuse to accept them as they are and stay angry as a way to keep some sense of hope that we will someday have a relationship with them, rather than face the finality of what is.

But you cannot make your parents different. They are who they are.

Letting go is about the relationship you have with them inside yourself.

No longer needing them.

What have you been getting out of not forgiving your parents?

What have you been getting out of holding on to the anger, and resentment?

Now, you might say "That's crazy, Kute. I am getting nothing out of it!"

But if you were getting nothing out of it, then you wouldn't be still holding on.

Sometimes, like Carolina, we hold on to old anger and resentment because we want to be right.

Sometimes we refuse to forgive because deep down, remaining angry is our unconscious way to somehow stay connected with them.

Sometimes we don't let go of the past because we are trying to protect ourselves. We don't want to forget so that we won't make that mistake again.

But don't you want to break free?

Take a moment and consider: What if your parents were no longer living?

Seriously. If your parents were no longer alive, would you make different choices for your life?

Often the answer is yes.

So you can choose now to let them go, and then you will

be able to live the life you want. Instead of spending your life angry and resentful, you can spend your life free.

When you let them go, you create a new life.

You've got to face your parents and forgive. Only then can you finally start to create something new.

CHAPTER | 4

LOSE YOUR MIND

One other thing is stealing your freedom.

It's not your parents. It's not your spouse. It's not your mortgage.

It's what you listen to all day long.

It's the soundtrack to your life.

It's your mind.

You've got to master the mind.

Or it will master you.

Running From It All

I was a chubby kid growing up. Okay, not chubby—I was fat. I got teased by all the kids in school, and even worse, was rejected by all the cute girls. I will never forget going shopping for a suit for my cousin's wedding. I was about nine years old. My cousin took me to every children's clothing shop in London, but nothing fit me. Eventually we had to buy a man's suit and have it tailored. It was one of the most embarrassing experiences of my life.

About a year later, I began reading the motivational literature of America. And in every new book I read, the mantra was clear. *You have the power to make big changes in your life. You can change your life and be everything you wish.* When I read those promises as a boy, feeling ashamed of how fat I was, how weird I was, how alone I was, I was inspired. I decided I was going to lose the weight. And I was going to start that day.

I walked out of the small house that we lived in behind my father's church. I decided I would run one time around the block. And I did. I ran slowly. It was painful. I was huffing and puffing the entire way. But I did it.

The next day I ran around the block twice.

Soon I was running around the block five times. Then running a mile, two, three, until I was running six miles a day.

And I ran every single day from the age of eleven to twenty-seven. I probably missed only four days in those sixteen years. Even when I was traveling, I would run. In the snow. In the mountains. When I had an early flight, I'd get up at two a.m. if I had to.

Running has saved my life in so many ways. Because running is about much more than the act of physical exercise and exertion; it is about the inner challenge of coming face-to-face with my perceived limitations. Running forces you to face your ideas of who you are, how far you can go physically, and how much strength you have within.

One cold London morning, when I was about fourteen and

out on my Saturday run, I just decided to keep running. To see how far I could go. My mind would be telling me, *This is it. You can't go any farther.* To stop. That it was too painful. But I would push that limit aside. In that moment, running became a meditation to transcend my limits. Would I believe the lie of my limitation? Or could I move through it? And not believe what I thought was the limitation?

Running taught me not to listen to the limitations of my mind. And that what I so easily perceived as my limits were actually not. They were an illusion.

That day I ran sixteen miles.

I know that my practice of running was one of the things that kept me sane when I first moved to America. The practice of getting up every single day and going running kept me focused on what was possible. Kept me from believing the many negative thoughts that might have driven me crazy or sent me running back home to London.

So I take people running in India.

Carlos was a real estate developer in his midthirties, married with two beautiful children. He was hugely successful financially. He had founded a large company, bought a mansion, an expensive car, and possessed all the trappings of a luxurious life. But he wasn't happy. His wife felt like he wasn't present in their marriage. She wanted more. He wanted more. He'd been going to seminars, reading books, working with coaches. But he still felt stuck. He said he was craving something deeper and hoped this journey would help him find that.

After a twenty-five-hour plane ride, we were exhausted and

spent another two hours driving around looking for a hotel. I could see that Carlos felt he had reached his limit. Enough was enough—he was ready to sleep. So as soon as we found a hotel, with a room that looked like a prison cell, I decided that it was time to go running.

We'd been awake for two days. It was probably about 90 degrees out in the burning hot sun. When I told him what we were going to do, Carlos looked at me as if I was crazy.

"Kute, I haven't gone running in . . . I don't know, ten years? I can't go running right now."

"Nope, c'mon, lace up your running shoes! It's time for a run."

He shuffled over to his bag, took out his sneakers, and put them on.

I knew he had no idea why this was the first thing we were going to do in India. Why not go to a nice cool temple and meditate for a bit, Kute? Why not go down and put our feet in the cold river, Kute?

No. When I want to push people to their limits, I know that running is one of the most direct ways to make that happen.

As Carlos and I began to run, it didn't take long before he became winded and exhausted. I knew he was tired, but I knew if I could get him to see how he could transcend his so-called limit *this* time, he'd never have an excuse again.

I ran by his side as we stepped over trash and wove through groups of children on our way out into the Indian countryside.

Carlos wanted to stop, to catch his breath; tears were streaming down his face. "I can't, Kute, please!" he cried.

Each time he stopped running, I would ask him, "Could you run right now?"

And as Carlos stood, hands on his knees, dripping with sweat, he'd say quietly, "Yes, I could."

"Then why aren't you running?" I asked, jogging in place.

"I don't know!" he said angrily.

I kept running and shouted over my shoulder: "Feel beyond it! Where are those thoughts that are telling you that you can't run anymore? Where are they? I want you to show me those thoughts. Because it's not about running, Carlos. It's about where your limit is."

I paused and turned around. He was still leaning over, but he looked up at me.

"It's about where your limit is, Carlos. Not your limit to run, but your limit to love. Those same feelings, voices, thoughts—that same mind pattern telling you that you can't run anymore is the one that says you can't love anymore. It's the one that says you can't open your heart anymore. It's telling you that you can't serve anymore. It's telling you to believe the limitation of who you are. But it's just the mind. Where does mind exist? Where do those thoughts exist? If you can show me those thoughts, I'll let you stop. But I want to see them."

Carlos took a deep breath. And then stood up and started shuffling toward me.

I let him catch up with me.

"Carlos, notice how those thoughts, those thoughts that don't actually exist, are actually controlling your body, are controlling your reality, are controlling your happiness. They are controlling you."

He started to jog in earnest now.

"Observe your mind. What's your mind telling you? If you listen to everything your mind tells you, you will never be free. It's telling you the same shit it has always told you. Watch your mind, smile at your mind; look at how it tries to get you to stop, how it's telling you to give up. It's telling you all these things, all of these false things. Observe your mind as it tries to convince you to listen."

We ran a few minutes in silence.

"Everything up to now was a warm-up. The place where you've reached your edge is where the run truly starts. Everything up until this point was you being in your comfort zone."

Now Carlos was no longer stopping every twenty feet but was starting to run at a good pace. I pushed him further. "The average person sees his limit and stops there. Limits are there to be overcome. To go beyond. Your limits are not as real as you think. This is how we become great, Carlos. We see our limits and we transcend them. It's what made the great ones great. They didn't accept their limits. They went beyond what anyone thought was possible."

We continued to run. We wound our way back through the streets to our hotel. When we finally stopped in front of it, Carlos turned to me, out of breath, exhausted, but exhilarated.

"Thank you," he said.

"You did it, Carlos. What is it that controls the body,

Carlos? The mind sends a message to the body, and your body is following. Following your mind will lead to big trouble. The mind should be a follower, not a leader. Your heart and spirit must be the leader. Then use your mind to figure out how to execute what the spirit and heart wants."

He nodded and we walked into the hotel. It was finally time for a shower and a rest. But our work had begun.

You are not your thoughts.

We've got to shed that layer. Thoughts are not who you are. You are so much bigger than your mind.

Static Quo

Stop and think about the power you give your mind.

You have more than 65,000 thoughts a day. Most are the same as yesterday. It's easy to get carried away with your thoughts. And before you know it, you're at their mercy.

Just because you have a thought doesn't mean it's real.

Again, just because you have a thought doesn't mean it's real.

Your thoughts are not real. They are just energy.

Your thoughts aren't the issue.

The importance you give your thoughts is the real issue.

Some of them are true. Many of them are lies. You can believe everything in your mind. You can become attached to your thoughts as important, essential, the truth. But you will be a prisoner.

Or you can choose to let them go.

You are so much more than your thoughts.

Every night on the banks of the Ganges, thousands of people gather to offer incense and gifts to the river, to chant and pray. One night Carlos and I went to watch the ceremony. As we stood there in the magical dusk of India, young children would come up to us, harassing us, poking us, pushing us, and prodding us to buy something. Carlos was trying to be reverent and experience the beauty of the ceremony, but the kids were really starting to annoy him. I told him, "Carlos, don't take them too seriously! Just as you take your thoughts and yourself too seriously. If you do, you'll just fuel them. Just smile, play with them. Then all of a sudden they'll leave because you don't offer resistance."

Our thoughts are like those kids. They just want attention. They just want to be taken seriously. When you start identifying with your thoughts and becoming attached to them as "real," you give them power. You've made them an issue.

You can continue living your life, believing every crazy thing that pops into your head, allowing your thoughts to control you. Or at any moment you can stop and observe your thoughts.

That is the key. Most of us get so tied up with our thoughts. We think they are us. But they're not, are they? You can observe what you are thinking. *Oh, I see, I'm thinking that I'm worthless right now.* Just that *act* of observing that thought provides some separation from the thought. If you can detach from the thought and observe it, then it is not you.

It is pure observation, without judgment. You must become aware and conscious of the thoughts that are arising. And then learn to question the thoughts. Rather than assuming every thought is true, pause and ask yourself, "Is it true? Is this thought true? Can I know this for sure?"

The mind spins a lot of fiction as reality. *He thinks I look fat. They think I'm stupid.* Do you really know those things? Are these facts? No. They are lies. You have no idea what others are thinking. At any moment you can refuse to buy into the lies your mind is spinning. If you can observe your thoughts but refuse to be owned by them, you can bring yourself back to center. You can achieve a level of mastery over the mind.

As the ceremonies began to wrap up, I decided I would give Carlos another test.

I said, "Are you ready to be a leader?"

He turned to me and nodded.

So I said with a smile, "Okay, you're going to lead the way back to the hotel now."

Carlos looked at me in surprise. At this point he had gotten very used to following me everywhere. So he didn't pay attention to where he was going; he just followed in my footsteps.

"Kute, how the hell am I going to do that? I don't know my way back. I have no idea where to go!"

I nodded. And said, "The only thing I am going to tell you is that we're going back to Rama Guest House."

He looked at me in frustration. And then began to look around, searching for something that looked familiar.

As soon as he began to walk, I followed just a few feet behind. But soon I started questioning him. "You don't know what you're doing, do you? Where are you going? You're too old for this. You're going down the wrong road. You're doing it wrong. Give up!"

Whenever he would pause at an intersection, I would start again. "Hmm, are you sure? Maybe you're taking the wrong turn?"

I was just showing him what his mind did to him all day long.

We walked in circles for hours. Carlos got increasingly frustrated. But eventually he found his way back to the hotel.

But not without me intentionally torturing him.

How much do you allow your thoughts to torture you?

Let's say a negative thought enters your mind.

I'm not good enough.

I'm too fat.

I'm not smart enough.

You can allow that thought to eat you alive. To squash any sense of self-confidence you have. To limit the way you live your life.

I won't ask her out.

I won't wear that dress.

I won't apply for that job.

But the thoughts aren't causing the problem.

The source of the problem is the importance you give to the thought. It's your *belief* in the thought.

I hate to tell you, but you will have negative thoughts. No one is immune from them. You probably have thousands of negative thoughts every day. If you try and fight with them, saying to yourself, *Don't think that! Stop it!* you just create resistance, which gives the thoughts more power, just like those street kids nagging Carlos.

Instead, when a negative thought emerges, don't stress about it. Don't get negative about the negative thought. Simply observe it and let it float by like clouds in the sky. A new thought will emerge.

Just like clouds in the sky, THOUGHTS WILL PASS.

The more you fight thoughts, the more power you give them. If you try and get rid of every negative thought, you will only drive yourself crazy. Instead, see them, acknowledge them, and recognize that they aren't real. That they don't need to drive the show. That you choose.

You choose. Whether to keep running or stop. Whether to stretch to your edge or stay where you are comfortable.

Stalking Steven Spielberg

I am not a stranger to these thoughts myself. My first few years in LA were some of the most difficult of my life. I had no money and no connections. I was working odd jobs here and there but didn't earn enough money to keep my apartment, so at one point I found myself couch surfing, dependent on the generosity of new friends. In order to eat, on occasion I would walk into a grocery store, fill a cart with random groceries, and push the cart around while eating a loaf of bread. Then I would abandon the cart and leave the store without paying for anything. But at least my belly was full.

This is not something I'm proud of. But back then it was the only way I knew how to survive.

Every day was a battle with my thoughts. Was I going to focus on my dreams or listen to the negative thoughts that told me I was crazy to move here, to try and make it, to keep going?

But there was something in that lack that paved the way for my dreams.

When you have nothing to lose, you have the freedom to risk it all.

Living in LA, I was exposed to media in a way I had never experienced in London. A cheap TV that I bought at a garage sale opened up a whole new world to me. Infomercials, talk shows, self-help seminars. And an idea got planted in my head.

My twenty-one-year-old self decided that he wanted to become the next Oprah Winfrey . . . but with a British accent.

I knew it was a lofty goal, a million miles from where I was. But I truly believed that I had been brought to America for a reason. And I was going to do everything I could to discover that reason.

I continued to read spiritual books, but I also started to read biographies of people I admired. People who had done bold things, things that no one expected them to do. One of those books was the autobiography of Steven Spielberg. I was deeply inspired by his commitment to what he wanted to do at a very young age. Many people thought he was too young, he needed to mature, he should wait for his time rather than go after big directing gigs and projects at the start of his career, but he pushed through, not willing to let other people limit his dream.

I finished the book and decided I wanted to meet him.

The negative thoughts in my head began to swarm, buzzing like angry bees. *You don't know anyone here. How are you going to find him? He's the most famous director in Hollywood! He won't give you the time of day.*

But what did I have to lose? Or I could spend another day eating free groceries at Vons.

I began to ask all the people I knew whether they had any connections to Steven Spielberg. And eventually I met a well-known producer who had worked with him. But when I asked him whether he would introduce me, he turned me down. However, he did offer me the phone number of his friend, a fellow who coached Spielberg's kids in soccer. I called that guy, who turned me down, too. But he felt some compassion for me and told me what park the games were played at on Saturday mornings.

I thought about it. Was it crazy to try and go down to this park on a Saturday morning and find Steven Spielberg?

Um, yes, it was crazy.

But instead of listening to that as a limitation, I turned it around. It was CRAZY to do this! But was I going to do it?

You bet.

We are often waiting for life to present the perfect opportunity, when life is actually waiting for US!

To do one simple thing.

So often people complain about their lack of resources. But this is an illusion. The reason your dream doesn't come true is never because you don't have enough money. It's because of a lack of resourcefulness, not resources.

Anyone can go to a soccer park on a Saturday morning in pursuit of a dream.

I put on my only suit, created a press kit with a four-page handwritten letter about what I dreamed of doing one day, and included a VHS tape of my one TV appearance on a local news station. I made two trips to the park. The first time, there was no sign of Spielberg. I'm sure the crowd of parents wondered who this strange-looking man was hanging out in a suit on the soccer fields on Saturday morning. But the second time, I spotted Spielberg from a distance. There he was. Right in that pack of parents was the man whom I had dreamed of meeting.

I totally froze. My heart was beating a mile a minute and my mind was screaming at me to run! But I knew if I listened to my mind, then I would let fear hijack my intention.

Spielberg was sandwiched in the middle of a group of

people walking back to their cars. The soccer game was over. It was now or never.

So I jumped in front of the entire group of people.

They all stood and stared in shock.

And then I just began to speak. "Mr. Spielberg, my name is Kute Blackson! I moved to America with nothing but the dream in my heart to inspire millions of people around the world, to help people reconnect with who they really are."

I began talking so fast I didn't even know what I was saying, giving my pitch about how I dreamed of becoming the next Oprah.

After a few moments his wife looked at him and grinned, and Spielberg chuckled.

"You know what?" he said with a smile. "You kind of remind me of myself at your age. How can I help you?"

I took a deep breath and talked to him about what I was working toward.

When I finished, he smiled again and said, "I like you. Give me your stuff and I'll take a look at it."

My hands were shaking as I handed over my press kit. I shook his hand and he began to walk away.

"Don't forget me, Mr. Spielberg!" I shouted after him.

Two days later, his office called me to set up a meeting with a major studio.

His office called me!

All because I dared to do something crazy and not listen to my mind, which was of course screaming that trying to meet Steven Spielberg was impossible.

A couple of weeks later, I met with some producers at Buena Vista Television, a division of Disney. They didn't know what to expect, just that Steven Spielberg had said to meet this young guy. And when Steven Spielberg says something, you listen.

Needless to say, they didn't quite get my vision of a new inspirational talk show.

They shook my hand, said no thanks, and sent me on my way.

But that didn't deter me. Because I had said I was going to meet Steven Spielberg, and I had MET Steven Spielberg! And he had seen the potential in me!

I had done the impossible. And when you have done the impossible, you just want to keep doing the impossible. I began to wonder what else I could do.

Once you transcend your limits, you see how pointless they really are.

All too often, our fears decide what we do, whom we talk to, what we go after.

But we don't have to let the idea that something is CRAZY stop us.

Yes, it is crazy. But isn't life crazy? Isn't craziness itself a kind of celebration of the excitement and mystery and miraculousness of life?

In that moment, when fear raised its head, I could have let it control me. I could have let it force me to turn around, retreat to the bus stop.

And then I would have lived my life wondering, *What if I'd just gone up to him and said something?*

The appearance of fear doesn't mean you should stop.

Fear can be a sign that you are growing and stretching outside your comfort zone. You are going into the unknown. Fear is a sign that you are at your edge. You are about to transcend your limits.

You don't have to let fear hijack your dreams.

You can turn to the part of you that is afraid and embrace it. Hold it. Acknowledge it. Thank it for caring enough to give you the signal to pay attention. And love yourself through that moment.

Do not let the fear stop you! Do not wait for the fear to be gone for you to take action.

It is a myth that you must become fearless.

True courage is the ability to embrace the fear and take action in spite of it.

That is the sign of true courage.

What If You Couldn't Fail?

What thoughts are you allowing to control you?

Don't let your mind be your master. When you stop letting fear be in charge, you begin to be able do more than you ever thought possible. You are able to access a whole new level of freedom because you refuse to allow your negative thoughts to be your constant companions, planting seeds of doubt about every courageous thing you dare to do.

Jennifer was the first woman I took to India. She had decided to work with me because despite having a very full life—a wonderful husband, three beautiful children, a big house, even a Ferrari—she felt empty inside. She walked into my office eight months' pregnant, unable to be alone, completely depressed, and addicted to cigarettes. "I can't find myself" was how she put it when we first began to work together.

After working together for a few months, we soon discovered that she couldn't find herself because deep down, she was ashamed of who she was. Jennifer had come to the United States from the USSR, and despite the fact that she had lived here for many years, she still had a heavy accent. She hated that it made her stand out and refused to speak in public because of it. In addition, Jennifer had been born dyslexic. And she allowed this to limit how far she reached in her professional endeavors. She lived in fear that if she had to write emails, people would know about her disability. So she didn't allow herself to go after her dream, which was to become a real estate agent.

She came to me out of the blue one day and looked straight in my eyes. "I am going to India with you, Kute. I am your next client! I know I must go."

I laughed, thinking she was joking.

She wasn't smiling. She just kept looking at me.

"I am going to India!" she said in her strong, serious, Russian-accented voice.

Her insistence was powerful. But I had never taken a woman on the Liberation Experience before. I wanted to be sure that this was right.

After I asked her to meditate on it for a few days, she came back as convinced as ever. And at this point I knew too—she was my next client for the Liberation Experience.

I knew from the start that my process would have to be a bit different with a woman. With men, I jump right in—either with tough questions or with a run on the banks of the river. But women are different. They work so hard to take care of others, striving to keep it all together, keep the family running, the business going, and the marriage working. So when we left for India, I wanted Jennifer to feel as if she was being taken care of, which would develop her trust in me. I needed to create a space so that she could relax and feel safe. A space where she felt like she didn't have to hold herself together anymore.

On the flight over, I sat behind Jennifer on the plane, as I usually do with my clients, giving her space. But I wanted her to know that I was there for her. The entire time. Every single second of the flight. Every so often, as I had expected, she would turn around and check on me. And instead of sleeping, as I usually do on these long journeys, I stayed awake so I could look back at her. Any time she'd turn around, I'd meet her eyes. I wouldn't say anything. But I tried to communicate: *I'm here. You can relax. I'm present. You can let go.*

And she did. We arrived in India and her eyes lit up with excitement. We began to do yoga and get her to truly be in her body again. We worked through some of the conditioning of her childhood and past. But I knew that the beliefs she had about herself, about what she could and couldn't do because of her accent, because of her "disability," were still in control.

The one thing that Jennifer told me she would NEVER do was jump off a cliff. She had been afraid of heights her entire life. She had decided that when she turned forty, she would skydive as a way to conquer this fear. But until then she was fine letting this fear limit her life.

One day we were traveling via rickshaw to the northern part of Rishikesh when I saw a van with WHITE WATER RAFTING written on the side; it was parked next to the road. I asked the rickshaw driver to pull over and got out. I walked down to the river, where a guide was setting up a raft for an expedition. "Do you have room for two more?" I asked. He nodded and told me the fee.

I ran back up the hill and told Jennifer we had a change of plans. We were going white-water rafting down the Ganges River.

I figured the river would be a great metaphor for life, for after all, in life there are times of calmness and beauty but also times of uncertainty and change.

But I soon realized there was a bigger reason we had been led to this river.

After about half an hour of paddling and taking in the Indian countryside, a part of the country people rarely get to see, away from the metropolis and highways, we came around a bend in the river, and there it was. A huge cliff about forty feet high. And underneath it, a swimming hole.

It had Jennifer's name written all over it.

I asked our guide if we might be able to stop for a swim. He nodded and guided us over to the banks of the river.

Jennifer looked at me. She knew what I had in mind.

"No way," she said firmly.

"What do you mean, no way? There is no way you could jump off that cliff? I know that's a lie. It's called gravity. It is a law of nature. If we climb up that hill, stare over the edge, and jump, you will fall. You will land in the water. You will swim over to the shore. You will have done it. So what do you mean, no way?"

We got out of the raft and stood looking up at the cliff. Jennifer didn't say anything. But I could sense the thoughts in her head.

I leaned over and whispered in her ear: "You know, Jennifer, the same mind that is telling you that you can't jump off this cliff is the same mind that has told you that you can't be a real estate agent. That you can't let anyone know about your dyslexia. That you can't let anyone hear your accent."

I paused.

"Those are just thoughts. You don't need to believe them. Can you observe them, acknowledge them, and then ask yourself if they are true?"

She took a deep breath. Her entire body was shaking with adrenaline.

"How about we climb the hill?" I asked.

She nodded.

Step by step we climbed up the steep embankment until we reached the top, where countless people were wildly throwing themselves off the cliff and splashing down into the water below.

We stood at the top. I didn't let Jennifer look down. I wanted her to leap unseeing into her future.

"What is your mind saying right now?" I asked as tears began to course down her cheeks.

"That this is crazy!" she said angrily.

"Yes, Jennifer, this is crazy! And isn't it wonderful?"

She stared at me like I was crazy too. And then she smiled at me through the tears.

We stood up there for two hours. Doing battle with her mind. (Thank God there were two rafts so one group could go ahead without us.)

But ultimately I helped her observe her thoughts. So she could realize that she had the power to take them or leave them.

Finally I could feel that she was ready to release it.

"You are ready, aren't you?" I asked with a grin.

She nodded.

"That's right," I said. "You are ready."

And she jumped.

I stared down as I watched her emerge from the water, triumphant.

I was screaming and cheering and jumping for joy.

This was the start of her shedding the layer.

Every day is an exercise in mastery over the mind. Every day we can believe the limitation. After an hour at the top of the cliff, *I* could have believed the limitation. *Okay, I'm pushing her too far here. We better just climb down this mountain and continue on the raft. That's enough of a test for her.*

But Jennifer was bigger than her mind.

There are so many moments in life in which we stand at the top of the cliff, staring over into the abyss, knowing that freedom comes from making the jump. And yet we turn away, walk back down the hill, and miss out on that moment of jubilation.

When do you allow your mind to limit what you accomplish? How long you stay? How hard you fight? How much you love?

What if you could consider those moments when you want to give up as an invitation to stretch into your greatness?

Right at the edge of your comfort zone is where the real growth begins. And where you find out what you are really made of.

One More Test

As we finished our rafting ride, Jennifer was still on a high from the adrenaline and the excitement of mastering her mind. But I knew that was just one fear of hers. Jennifer was letting so much limit her that we needed to keep going and tackle a fear that was doing much more to limit her life than her fear of heights.

The next day we drove for several hours to a remote school. I told Jennifer on the ride that the children who attended this school came from all over the country and lived miles away from their families in hopes of going to college after they graduated. Now, for these children, the dream of going to college is like a dream of going to the moon. It is so far from their reality. And yet they dare to dream big. They dare to see past the many limitations standing in their way.

As children, we have not yet been conditioned to believe lies.

When we pulled into the school, hundreds of children were gathered in a big room to meet us. I stood up and said a few words. And then I handed the microphone to Jennifer.

"Now it is your turn."

She looked at me with terror. "Kute, what do you mean?"

"I want you to go up there and talk to these children. You came to America from Russia. You've done amazing things in your life. And now you are here. Tell them about what is possible. You can do it."

Jennifer looked as if she might faint.

"What's important is not what you say or how you say it. What's important is your energy, your heart, your soul. Share it with them and you cannot fail."

All of Jennifer's negative thoughts were wreaking havoc in her head. I could see it.

All I said was "You can."

And then she took the microphone from my hand. I sat down. She looked at me again.

"You can," I said again with a smile. "Remember the cliff?"

She nodded.

"This is a test. You can go back to living according to the lies of the mind. Or you can remember how you shed that layer."

And she began to speak.

It was a beautiful moment. No, her words weren't perfect. Yes, she had an accent. But her accent was a reflection of where she came from. Her accent was a symbol of how far she had come. She spoke about fleeing the USSR as a young girl, first going to Israel and then to America. She spoke about how important it is to never give up, no matter what. To keep working and dreaming and hoping. At the end of her speech, the children surrounded her with hugs and kisses and kind words. She looked as if her heart would burst with joy.

She had dismantled one of the limiting beliefs that she had been allowing to dictate the course of her life.

Let me tell you something about Jennifer. When she came back to America, she no longer allowed her beliefs to prevent her from moving forward in her life. She started her own real estate company, which grew into an empire. She began to speak in public. She now speaks at least once a month to thousands of people. Real estate agents who want to build something great with their lives come to listen to Jennifer speak about her experiences.

Just three months after she got back from India, she did an ultramarathon.

She ran forty-five miles!

She truly believed that every moment was an opportunity to overcome.

Your mind will take all your power if you let it.

It will dictate everything, from the choices you make to the people you love to the capacity you have to be truly happy.

Are You Happy Right Now?

Let's go back to Carlos. A few days into our trip, I took him to Dharavi, one of the largest slums in all of Asia. More than a million people live there. Located right in the hub of downtown Mumbai, it's a city within a city. It is so tightly packed with makeshift shacks that neither taxis nor rickshaws can maneuver its narrow alleyways. Many of the people who live here have lived here for generations, several generations dwelling within one small hut. When people hear "slum," they think of very poor people. But within Dharavi, there are bustling businesses within the tin walls of the shacks. There are chai stalls, embroidering companies, soapmaking shops, and bakeries. It is unlike anything in the world.

We were going to visit my friend Vijay. We walked carefully through the crazy Mumbai traffic and then through the narrow streets of the slum. It is easy to get lost in Dharavi. But finally I saw the familiar doorway of Vijay's house. He was waiting for us.

"Kute!" he yelled with excitement as we embraced. I introduced Carlos.

Vijay bowed and took Carlos's hand. "This is my house. Welcome," he said with pride.

We walked in. I saw Carlos take in the living conditions.

We were standing in a tiny eight-by-ten-foot room. In it sat Vijay's entire family—his wife, his two children, and his parents. They rose to greet us with huge smiles on their faces. His wife offered us cookies and soft drinks. I knew that many of the people who live in Dharavi live off one to two dollars a day. I couldn't take more, but his wife kept insisting.

Carlos had been quiet as he watched the family's interactions.

Finally he spoke up. "Vijay, you look happy. Here, with your beautiful family, you seem happy. Are you, Vijay? Are you truly happy?"

And Vijay looked at him with a confused expression on his face. "Happy? Why, we must to be happy. We simply must to be happy."

And then he turned around to serve his parents.

As we left that evening and walked back to our hotel, Carlos was quiet.

"It's quite life-changing, isn't it?" I said.

Carlos nodded.

"In America, we live with so much, and we can't find it within us to be happy. We think we need all of these things to be happy. Vijay, he shows us true freedom, doesn't he?"

Carlos stopped in the street and turned to me. "Kute, I've been searching for so long for the happiness, the peace that they had in that room. In the midst of the biggest slum in the world. And they had everything! They had everything," he said sadly.

And right there in the street, he began to cry.

"It was just in my mind, wasn't it?" he asked.

"What, Carlos?"

"The lack, the need. It was all in my mind. I have had everything I've needed all along. To be happy. To be free."

"Yes, Carlos, yes. Perhaps the real slum is not a physical place but a state of mind. When we are focused on what is not working, what we don't have, or are stuck in fear, in that moment, we are living in the slum of our mind, even while we are living in the nicest mansion in the world."

I put my hand on his shoulder. He looked into my eyes.

"But, Carlos, when you realize that you can shed that layer, that you have the power to CHOOSE to listen to your mind or to let it go, then you have the power to realize that outer circumstances do not determine your inner freedom or happiness."

He nodded and gave me a hug. There in the middle of the slums of India, we embraced. In gratitude for the realization that could set us both free.

When you shed the layer of the mind, you realize you have spent your life fighting the voices in your head.

It's time to let them go. It's time to push past the limitations your mind wants to place on you.

Because when you are the one, you realize there is no limit to what you can do, who you can become, how happy you can be, and where your life can go.

You are not your thoughts. Your thoughts will come and go. When you remove them from their seat of power, you finally can take back the reins of your life.

CHAPTER | 5

THE ROAD TO NOWHERE

Did you know that you are always exactly where you are supposed to be?

Even when you think you are not?

It's your ego that thinks you should be somewhere else doing something else with someone else as someone else.

The ego is constantly searching for something. Its job is to seek but never to find.

So we often spend our lives seeking, searching for something that always seems just over the horizon.

Maybe you are searching for your purpose. Your self. Your soulmate.

But what do you think will be different once you find that?

This moment right now is no different from that moment in the future.

Right now you are exactly where you are meant to be.

This very moment is IT.

This very moment is the most amazing moment of your life . . . if you are open to its miracle.

Slow the F Down

After Carlos and I had been in India for about a week, we were sitting and eating some breakfast at a train station. I began to watch Carlos eat. Bite by bite, Carlos was stuffing his mouth with food. He would barely chew a bite before shoving another into his mouth. There was no way he could even be tasting the flavors of the food, its textures. Was he even aware of what he was eating? He didn't even seem to be aware of where we were, what we were doing.

I leaned over and I put my hand on his arm and said, "Carlos, is that how you make love to your wife?"

This comment was met with dead silence.

Now, this wasn't out of nowhere. Intimacy was one of the issues that Carlos and his wife had been struggling with before coming to India. But Carlos still looked at me stunned, as if he had been punched. I smiled, a twinkle in my eye.

"Carlos, if that is how you've been making love to your wife, can you see why maybe she might not be inspired to be with you? As you are eating, I see how unconsciously you go about it. You are not present with the food. You do not taste the food. You are checked out, in a kind of trance. Now, I don't really care about the food itself, but what I want you to notice is how you experience life moment to moment. I couldn't care less about how you eat, other than 'HOW' you eat. I feel it is reflecting how you're making love. How you're making love is reflecting how you're living. Everything is interconnected."

Carlos set down his food. He swallowed the bite that remained in his mouth. He gazed out the window and ran his hand over his head.

He began to nod slowly.

"You're right. I'm not present when I eat. That's why I'm thirty pounds overweight. What we've eaten in the last couple of days has been the equivalent of one or two meals at home. When I eat back home, I don't even notice what I put in my mouth. I just keep eating."

"Carlos, if you want to have the relationship that you truly want, you've got to learn to be present in your life. While you eat, while you make love. So from now on, when we eat, I would like you to chew each bite thirty-three times."

"Thirty-three times?" Carlos asked, incredulous.

"Yes, thirty-three times."

He nodded and picked up his fork again. And began to eat.

Throughout the breakfast I kept my eye on him. And I would ask, "How many times was that, Carlos?"

"Hmm, I don't know."

"That was twenty-four. Be present with the food. Be present. Be present with your actions, be present with your breath, be present with life, be present with your wife. Meditation is not simply something that you do on a cushion once a day. It is something you do moment to moment. Live moment to moment with total awareness. Life itself is meditation."

Confused, Carlos looked at me. "But my wife is not here, Kute," he said with a smile.

"No, Carlos, she is not, but how you are in this very

moment is how you are with her at home. Learn to be here so you can learn to be with her, truly be with her, when you go home."

Soon this practice transcended our eating. But every meal I made him count how many times he chewed each bite. Thirty-three. Never less. Never more.

Finally, on the last day as we were about to leave India, we arrived at the airport and I bought us some samosas to eat before getting on the plane. I picked one up and then offered Carlos the other. We stood and ate them at the counter.

We ate in silence. Until I heard Carlos let out a loud scream. And he pulled from his mouth a long, sharp piece of clear glass that he had bit into.

He dropped it onto the plate and shook his head in complete disbelief.

He looked at me and we both laughed in shock. "Holy shit, had I not been practicing chewing my food thirty-three times, I would have swallowed that thing and it would be in my stomach."

He paused now, aware of the gravity of what had just happened. "Kute, by the time I got on the plane, I could have been bleeding internally and then stuck over the ocean with no one to help. I could have died!"

"That is true, Carlos. India gave you one last lesson. This moment is the most important of your life. Now. And now. And now."

After I watched Carlos walk onto the plane, I shook my head. I remembered all too well what it was like to rush through the moment, caught up in getting someplace else, so much so that you lose the ability to notice what is happening right in front of your face.

It happens to all of us. We start to get checked out of our lives. Maybe we are trying to avoid something uncomfortable. Maybe we aren't inspired. Maybe we are busy; we are working so hard to keep up that we miss the moment right in front of us. Maybe we are hiding behind a screen, wrapped up in the virtual world and missing what truly matters.

Take a look at your life. Where are you truly not present?

It's time to wake up and realize that right in front of us is the only moment of our lives. This is the layer. We must learn to shed our obsession with getting someplace else.

There is nowhere but right now.

Midlife Crisis

My awakening to this truth came in an unlikely place a few years earlier. It came on a simple road in northern Spain called the Camino de Santiago.

The Camino de Santiago is a 500-mile walk through northern Spain, through the Pyrenees beginning in the South of France and ending where the remains of the apostle James are said to be buried in the town of Santiago de Compostela, Galicia. It is the world's most famous spiritual pilgrimage. Among the people who have traveled its course are Saint Francis of Assisi, Charlemagne, Chaucer, and Dante.

I traveled to the Camino when I was twenty-three years

old. I had been in LA for five years. And yet despite my encounter with Spielberg, him setting up a meeting for me with his production company, and getting connected with the very spiritual teachers whom I had come to learn from, I still felt as if I was tapping into only a fraction of my potential. I was playing small when I was ready to play big.

I had continued to reach out to other entertainment managers, hoping they might seize the opportunity to partner with me. I called, sent letters, knocked on doors. Usually I heard nothing. And then suddenly one of them responded. I was invited to come to their new offices. They had just begun a new firm and were looking to add new talent.

I couldn't believe it. These guys represented some of the biggest names in the world. And they had just set up a meeting with me.

When I walked into their offices, I looked around. They were so new that they didn't even have office furniture yet. We had to sit on the floor in the conference room. It wasn't exactly how I had envisioned things. But I gave my pitch to one of the managers. At the end he looked a bit stunned and then said quietly, "Give me a moment. I want you to meet my partner." I did the entire pitch again, this time for his partner. They spoke out in the hallway for a few minutes. And then they walked back in with hands outstretched to shake mine. "Okay, we want to sign you. We think you have what it takes, and we know exactly what to do with you to make you a big star."

I was flabbergasted. I couldn't believe it. After so much rejection, I was just used to it. And now someone was saying yes!

They said they were going to draw up the contract and then they would be in touch about my coming in to sign it. I hardly knew what to say, but I shook their hands vigorously, saying, "Thank you! Thank you!"

As I drove home, I still couldn't believe it. Here it was, everything I'd been striving for. A chance to reach millions of people. These managers would be able to open doors I never could.

But as the car made its way through the traffic of La Cienega, I couldn't ignore it.

There it was again. My soul speaking to me.

And this time its voice was clear. It said no.

Now, this was the very soul that had led me here, to America. My soul had never led me wrong.

But why no? Why now? I'd been rejected so many times, and now someone was going to say yes, and my soul says, "No, wait, these are not the right people to represent you."

Saying no to this deal was crazy!

But I had started this journey committed to not compromising what my soul was telling me, so I had to continue trusting that there must be a better way.

I called them up the next day and said that I couldn't sign the contract.

They were shocked, at a complete loss for words. Here I was, this nobody who had knocked on their door. Out of the kindness of their hearts, they listened to my pitch. And they were giving me a chance. Who was I to say no?

And I felt the same way! I didn't have any good reason,

except that my soul didn't feel like it was the right choice for me.

They hung up.

I began to lose faith. I couldn't see the path in front of me. I just felt like I was in the dark. Why come so far only to say no to that offer? My ego was making me question my soul.

A few days later, I was driving down to San Diego to interview a leader in the spiritual community.

While I was driving, I started praying intensely in my car. (I can't imagine what it looked like to the people around me.) I had been in America for five years, and yet in this moment, I felt like it had all been for nothing. I knew I was right to have listened to my soul. But I still felt like I was supposed to be doing something more than what I was doing. So I prayed: "God, what do you have planned for me? What is my purpose? I don't understand why you would have me turn that deal down. Please, you need to guide me on what to do next."

I sat there in my car, speeding down the highway, hoping for a response. And it came.

But it certainly wasn't what I was expecting.

I "heard" a voice say, Do the Camino.

Excuse me?

Be careful when you ask the universe for guidance.

It never responds in the way you expect.

I did not know why God would want me to walk the

Camino. But he soon made it crystal clear that he was leading me there.

At first I was confused by this so-called sign. I didn't know how it could ever happen. First, I didn't have the money, either to travel to Spain or to take several months off from work. It seemed ridiculous to step away while I was in the midst of building a business. Second, I was afraid. Not only is it a physically taxing journey, it is also notorious for its transformative powers. Because the entire route is along a ley line, or a mystical force field, the Camino is described as the kind of pilgrimage that has the power to truly upend lives. Was I ready for that?

I didn't know.

A few days later, I was having dinner with my best friend, and I told him about how I had decided to do the Camino, even though I had no idea financially how I could make it happen.

He listened intently.

"Do you really feel guided to do this?"

"Yes! I mean, I have never had such a strong feeling before that I was being guided to do something. It reminds me of those days in London, when I knew I wanted to come to America, but just didn't know how. The Camino? I'm not sure how it will happen. But I know there is a way," I insisted.

"How much would you need to do it?" he asked.

"I have no idea," I replied. I hadn't actually thought about how much it would cost to buy a plane ticket, not to work for several months, and to have money to keep me going on the trail.

He pulled something out of his bag and was writing on it under the table. He then pushed a piece of paper toward me on the table.

I turned it over and it was a check. For $10,000.

I stared at the check in amazement.

"You're going to lend me $10,000?" I asked in disbelief.

"No," he replied. "I feel guided to do this. I'm going to give you a gift of $10,000."

"You don't want me to pay you back?" I said, incredulous.

"No, it's a gift," he confirmed. He paused, took a drink of water, and then said, "Look, you know I feel conflicted about working for a company I hate. Yet I've been given stock in the company and it's gone through the roof. I sit here with money in the bank that I don't feel like I've really earned. So I'm going to give it to you."

I was speechless as tears welled in my eyes. Finally I was able to sputter, "Thank you. I'll be eternally grateful. I won't let you down."

"Don't consider it a gift from me, but a gift from God," he said.

This was yet another example of taking a leap of faith and the universe supplying exactly what I needed. First it was my green card. Now this.

I truly believe that when you move forward in faith, the universe is waiting for you. Many of us want miracles to happen in our lives, but we don't take the first step.

Say yes, and the way will unfold.

So I bought my ticket, packed a small backpack, and landed in Madrid. I took a train and a taxi to the small town of Saint-Jean-Pied-de-Port, where the trail begins. I registered in the small church that manages the nonstop parade of pilgrims arriving each day. By that afternoon I was on the trail.

I stood looking at the path in front of me. "Okay, God," I prayed. "Here we go."

The Spiritual Ironman

I hadn't done a lot of research before the trip. In some ways, I was scared. I would be walking for a month or so, completely and totally alone. It reminded me of that moment when I landed in LA, knowing no one. There would be no one there to distract me from my thoughts, from my fears, from my prayers.

I had learned where the trail started and where you can stay along it. But I didn't realize that there were two different paths you could take to get to the first stop on the trail. One ran along the highway and was completely flat. The other went straight up the mountain.

You can imagine which one I took.

I walked twelve miles that day. Straight up the mountain. In deep, dense fog. I could barely see the path in front of me.

Well, this isn't very subtle, I thought with a smile. Here I've been feeling like God has kept me in the dark, and where do I find myself? In the freakin' dark.

I arrived at the hostel that night exhausted but exhilarated.

Twelve miles. And that was up some of the steepest terrain I'd ever hiked. If I could average more like twenty miles a day on flat terrain, I'd be done in less than a month!

When I woke up the next morning my legs were so stiff it hurt to move them. It was like someone had taken a knife and sliced repeatedly through my thighs.

But my ego said, *Forget it. You're an athletic guy. You can do this. You go running every day of your life. You can handle a bit of hiking.*

I got back on the trail. About midway through the day, I saw some fellow pilgrims on the path ahead of me.

I blitzed right past them. Like I was in some sort of spiritual Ironman, out to win the race. I felt such pride. I didn't see the irony that pride is quite the opposite of the point of a spiritual journey.

By the day's end, I became aware of every aching muscle in my body. But I'd hiked twenty miles that day. Mission accomplished!

I woke up the next day barely able to move.

Okay, this was day three. I'd now covered thirty-two miles. I still had four hundred and sixty-eight to go.

Maybe I need to slow down a bit, I thought.

I hobbled to the shared bathroom of the hostel and hunched over the sink. I washed my face and dried it, trying to determine how I was going to keep going today.

And as I looked in the mirror, I found a kind old face staring back at me.

I turned around to find a man smiling at me in sympathy.

He put his hand gently on my shoulder and said, "My friend, have you ever done anything like this before?"

At first I felt confused. What, did I really look that bad? Did I really need his sympathy?

But ultimately, I knew he was probably here to encourage me. I shook my head. "No," I said quietly.

"It's okay, my friend. This journey is hard. Why do you think it's such a famous pilgrimage? Because it will expose every part of you as you struggle to complete it. But let me give you one piece of advice." Here he paused. "Love your feet. Every two hours stop, rest them, massage them, take off your shoes and socks and let your feet get some sun. Believe me, it will be worth it in the long run, even though you may not finish quite as fast."

I felt the truth of his statement deep in my bones.

I smiled at him and thanked him for his advice. He shuffled out of the bathroom.

I stared at myself in the mirror.

I knew I needed to heed his advice or I would never make it the entire five hundred miles.

Before I left for Spain, I heard one refrain over and over: How you do the Camino is how you do life.

And when you think about how I had hiked those first two days on the trail, there was one theme. I hadn't stopped walking until I reached what I thought was the destination. A certain hostel or monastery along the trail. Sometimes I would reach one and consider how much farther it was to the next one; then I would decide to keep going so as to make it farther that day. From sunup to sundown, I just kept hiking. Rushing to get to the next destination.

I sat down on a bench outside the bathroom and thought about my life back home. About how focused I was on achieving my life goals by the time I was twenty-five. How obsessed I was about what God's purpose was for my life.

I was so focused on why I thought I was here on this planet that I was missing why I was here on this planet.

I had a profound thought.

What if there is nowhere to get to?

What if this very moment was the most important moment of my life?

I was so worried about my purpose, about achieving my goals, that I was missing out on LIFE. There was nowhere to get to on the Camino except the end. It wasn't a race. The end wasn't a finish line. No prizes were passed out at the end.

The prize was each moment on the trail.

This lesson changed me profoundly.

Often, in our striving to get somewhere, we lose the fact that we are here.

Right here.

Nowhere else.

Think about it. Where is your attention focused most days? Making partner? Training for a marathon? Finding your spouse? Getting pregnant? Winning the prize? Making a million?

What do you think will be different about your life when you reach X, Y, or Z?

Nothing will be different. Except that you missed out on all the moments in between.

What would you do right now if there was nowhere to get to?

We've got to peel back the layer that is convinced there is somewhere to get to. Stop. Look around.

You are already here. The journey is the reward. Every step is the destination.

The Waiting Room

It's time for us to wake up and realize just how much of our lives we spend waiting. Waiting to accomplish the goal. Waiting to meet the right person. Waiting to make enough money. Waiting to reach retirement.

We somehow think that life doesn't start until we reach a certain destination.

Take Arthur. When I took Arthur to India, he was a complete control freak. Back home he ran a successful business; he was a CEO with thousands of employees. In fact Arthur was more than just the CEO; he essentially did everyone's job for him or her. No one performed as well as Arthur.

He and his wife have seven kids. So they ran a tight ship in order to get every child to the right extracurricular activity at the right time. It was a complicated dance of schedules and pickups and negotiations.

But of course India didn't allow Arthur any of that control.

One afternoon we arrived at the airport and soon discovered that our flight to Lucknow was delayed. At first it was delayed forty minutes. Soon it was delayed an hour. And then four hours.

Now, I've found that observing people at the gate of a delayed flight is a lesson in itself. People begin to get incredibly frustrated. Today was no different. I looked around the crowded area. Everywhere I looked I saw angry and unhappy people. I observed Arthur reacting the same way. He was slouching over, closing his eyes, simply waiting, waiting, waiting, to get on the plane.

I walked over and sat down next to Arthur. "What are you waiting for, Arthur? This waiting is also life. You're waiting to get on a plane to go to some destination. Just because the plane is delayed, you think this isn't life. That when you get there, it will somehow be *more* of life than this moment. That *that* is more than *this*. Like there is somewhere to get to."

I paused and looked around. Arthur did the same.

"We think that real life is something that happens when you arrive. When you get married, when you have a child, when you get the girlfriend or job or book contract—whatever *it* might be. When in reality, life is *this* right now, even in this waiting. We think that over there is more *it* than this. This is as *it* as it gets. Arthur, this is *it*."

Arthur stared at the suffering going on around us.

As we looked around the crowded room, we started to laugh. It was hilarious to watch how these people were waiting.

"How we wait reveals how we live life. We often think, *Oh, I'm just waiting. What does it matter?* But it actually reveals how we live life itself. When you give up waiting, you can actually start living life now as it really is."

Arthur smiled. "Kute, you are right. Here we are. We are here. There is nowhere to get to. What shall we do, then, with right now?" he asked with a twinkle in his eye.

Boom! Exactly, Arthur. Exactly.

What are you waiting for? When are you so focused on getting someplace else that you have missed the moment in front of you?

So shed the layer. There is nowhere to get to.

What are you left with?

Right now.

So breathe. Look around. Experience this moment fully. It doesn't cost any more to enjoy it fully. There's no rule that says you can't enjoy each moment until you arrive at some goal or destination. There is nothing wrong with the goal! But if you are waiting to truly live until you have accomplished it? You miss out on life.

Feel the simple reality that right now you are alive. You are alive. It's only when you are about to die that the preciousness of this simple moment becomes clear. So why not experience it now?

We knew this truth when we were born. Before you were conditioned to look ahead, plan for the future, achieve all these things, there was nowhere to go except bike riding with your best friend. There was nothing to do except skipping rocks on the lake. There was nothing to be except you.

But as we go through life, we are conditioned to believe that there are all these things we are supposed to be, all these things we are supposed to do. College. Career. Marriage. Kids. We make life complicated when it is really simple. We think our life is all about reaching those goals, and then we will have arrived.

But when we get caught up in those pursuits, we miss what life is really about.

Why Are We Here?

A few years ago, I visited Egypt and spent some time exploring the Pyramids. When I went inside, I saw where Pharaoh Tutankhamun (King Tut) was buried. It was a huge space. King Tut had made sure all of his treasures were buried with him. His gold, his silver, his jewelry. All of his riches, he wanted in his tomb. He planned to take them with him into the afterlife.

The next day I went to the Egyptian Museum in Cairo and found myself on a floor that was entirely devoted to the treasures King Tut had had buried with him in his tomb. And there it all was: gold chairs, gold bags, gold rods, gold necklaces, jewelry, and crowns. They had excavated it from his tomb and put it all on display. It was endless. Unimaginable! I'd never seen so much gold in my life!

At first I was in awe. I just couldn't believe the amount of gold that the pharaohs had actually buried with them in their tombs. But then a profound thought hit me: Tutankhamun was dead and his gold was still right here.

It was still here. And he wasn't.

No matter what you accumulate—houses, cars, watches, jewelry, even gold—when all is said and done, we take none of it with us, NOTHING at all!

We are all born the same and we all die the same. When you die, your true soul's bank account will become evident.

The only thing you take with you is the evolution of your soul and who you became in the process of life.

I am all for abundance and prosperity on the material plane. However, what's the use of big houses, fancy cars, and elaborate trinkets and gold if in the pursuit of them, you forget about your very soul? You step on others and become someone you are not? If you die and have amassed billions but didn't grow at all, then you really were the poorest man or woman in the world.

When we understand that, our whole definition of success changes.

You have to remember what the game is all about. You can have a million dollars and still be a total failure.

That's right! You can have a million dollars or a billion dollars and still be a total failure!

Because it's not about the bank account. It's about who you are becoming.

What's happening on the surface is only one level. What's happening inside you is what's real. And when you shift inside, then you will alter what happens outside.

I've had clients who have been in what appeared to be the perfect marriage. But they come to me and are deeply unhappy. They don't feel loved. They don't feel heard. They don't feel the freedom to be themselves.

They could stay in the marriage. It may look like a success on the outside.

But it is a failure to their soul.

If they find the courage to see what attracted them to the wrong person to begin with or what caused their initial closeness to dissolve, they can either right the marriage or step away and get a divorce. Now the world thinks, *Oh no! A divorce! What a failure!*

But is it? If the people in that marriage are finally set free? Can finally be who they really are? Can find their authentic selves?

To me, that relationship was a success. Because it helped each partner evolve, grow, and move on to the next level of life.

You can choose to view life as a random set of experiences that are happening to you—which sets you up to be a powerless victim. Or you can chose to view life as a school, and then every experience provides an opportunity for growth. Every moment is a chance to become more of who you truly are. This is real success—soul success. The degree to which you were true to your soul and what it was seeking to experience in this human incarnation.

My clients learn this in India. When I say I don't have an itinerary, I really *mean* I don't have an itinerary. Because I know that life will bring about situations that will cause them to face their issues. I don't need to go looking for lessons. Lessons come to us. Every day, every moment, is a lesson in itself.

Life Lessons

One such soul session happened as Clark and I were sitting watching life go by in India, so different from daily life in the West. Shopkeepers selling cheese, tea, silk shawls, and everything in between. Narrow streets filled with pilgrims who came to Varanasi to pray and bathe in the Ganges.

And then there were the cows. They just stood there in the middle of the narrow streets. Like "Yeah, I am cow. What are you going to do about it?"

They just stood there. Owning it. And people revered them.

As we were sitting there, we talked about Clark's relationship with animals. Just a few days earlier, I had asked Clark to recount one of the funniest moments of his life. And he told me the story of growing up on the farm and having to chase coyotes away from the chickens. He told a story of beating one of the coyotes who kept coming back. And as he described this experience with glee, I felt like something was off here. I didn't say anything, but I stored it away in my mind. There was some work to be done.

He had also described how when he got back home, he wanted to go hunt a bear so he could put the head of the bear on the wall. He thought it would look cool.

Now, Clark had grown up in a household where hunting was just the way of life. And I wasn't one to judge the habits of his family. But the joy that he took in the killing—that was troubling. You could say his relationship to animals wasn't one of reverence.

As we were talking about his hobby of hunting, a cow turned toward us. And starting walking in our direction.

I had the sneaking suspicion that this cow was here for Clark.

The cow stopped right in front of us, blinking lazily, not looking directly at us, but standing sideways so her entire body blocked our path and we were staring at her profile.

After a few moments of just standing in front of us, she decided to sit down. In the middle of the road.

I could feel a soul moment was about to happen.

I looked at Clark. And said, "I think there is a reason this cow is sitting here."

And as I said that, the cow turned and stared at Clark and flapped her ears. Clark stared back.

"There is a reason this cow is here. I think this cow is trying to tell you something. I want you to sit here with this cow until you know what it is trying to tell you."

Clark sat quietly in front of the cow.

After a few moments he said, "I think the cow is trying to tell me . . . 'Respect me.' "

The moment he said that, the cow turned and looked at him and flapped her ears again.

"Yes, Clark. It feels that way, doesn't it? It feels like in some way you haven't really respected animals."

As I said this, tears began to stream down Clark's face.

"I haven't. I mean, I haven't even told you . . ." He hiccupped as he tried to speak through his tears. "I don't think it was intentional, but that's just how it was done. I killed them, shot them, hunted them, hit them. I've inflicted so much pain on animals without even thinking about it."

We remained seated on the ground.

"Now is your chance, Clark. This cow represents all the animals that you have mistreated in your life. She is saying that you can now make a different choice. You can ask for her forgiveness, learn the lesson, and walk away from here a different person."

Clark nodded and did his best to confess to this cow, this holy animal, the ways that he had wronged her species.

And after that, the cow got up off the ground and walked away.

It was as simple as that.

Clark had evolved. As he got to know who he really was, he got in touch with the sacredness and oneness of ALL of life. He realized that we are all one and inextricably interconnected.

He had evolved as a soul.

This is why we are here on the planet. To evolve.

All around us are moments where we can face the old way we've done things and choose to take the higher ground the next time around.

The next day, as we were walking back to the guesthouse where we were staying, the most strange and amazing thing happened. We crossed a crowded intersection, with cars and people coming in every direction. And yet smack in the middle of it was another cow. Cows in the street are just part of the atmosphere of India, so bikes, cars, people, and motorcycles just cruised past this cow without a second thought. But as we approached, people started to scatter and I heard a loud scream—it was from Clark. Other screams rang out and everyone ran in different directions. I saw Clark be pushed across the intersection.

I ran over to him when I saw a large gash in his shirt.

The cow had charged him, and one of her huge horns had pierced his chest.

I pulled Clark over to the sidewalk and examined his wound. Luckily it was just a scrape, only a small amount of blood. We determined no ribs were broken. And while he was in pain, Clark was shaking his head, in shock, in pain, in confusion.

But I knew this was not random. This was the universe at work.

"Clark, why do you think this happened? There must be

a reason. Of all the people here in this crowded intersection, you're the one who gets hit by the cow." Clark turned to look at me. "But, Kute, I don't understand. I apologized yesterday to the cow."

"Well, it's no accident that the cow picked you out, Clark."

"I was minding my own business," he said, still in shock.

"Yes, but think about it, Clark, so were those animals when you hit them."

He nodded solemnly. "Now I know what it's like to be on the receiving end."

"Perhaps the cow of the universe wanted to show you what it's like to be on the receiving end. Even though the cow gave you only a little punch with its horns, it hurt and shocked you."

I paused.

"If you get the message, we can complete this chapter."

He looked up at the sky, completely humbled. "I get the lesson. I won't do it anymore. If that's anything like how it feels for the animals that I have hurt, I will never hurt another animal ever again."

We walked back to the guesthouse, shaken but changed.

A couple of days later, I told Clark, "You know, you may want to think twice before you kill that bear for no reason, just to put his head on your wall."

He turned to me. "I already thought about that. I ain't gonna be killing no bears. I'm done with that."

I smiled and patted him on the back. I was grateful that

this one shift in one person would impact animals all across the planet.

As you transform yourself, you don't do it just for yourself, but for every human being on the planet.

The universe is waiting to teach you if you are just open to her lessons.

When you begin to understand that you are brought to this planet to grow and evolve, you can truly begin to see everything and everyone as your teacher. Every experience is a vehicle to help you evolve. When you can see the bigger purpose, you realize that while we get caught up in the stuff that is happening on the surface—a gash from a cow, a divorce, an illness, a job loss, winning the lottery—it's what is happening underneath, in your soul, which counts.

So when you find yourself asking, *Why did I end up in this relationship? Why did I lose my job? Why did I have to go through this betrayal? Why is this cow blocking my way?*, this is a great moment. Look for the lesson within it.

Often the most challenging experiences of your life are the greatest catalyst for your soul's growth. Welcome them.

Take a look at your life right now. Examine those situations that are causing you pain and frustration. You may be asking, *Why is this happening to me? What did I do wrong to deserve this?*

This is a victim mentality that will only keep you stuck.

Take a look at your situation, and instead of asking, *Why is this happening to me?* ask yourself, *Why did I attract this situation? What is my soul seeking to learn? How can I grow from this?*

All lessons will be repeated until we learn them fully. You didn't do anything wrong. No one put a curse on you. Simply, in order to graduate and go on to the next level of our lives, we must learn the lesson. If we don't learn the lesson inherent within the situation or relationship, we actually keep ourselves stuck. Let me repeat: **We keep ourselves stuck.**

YOU. ME. NO ONE ELSE.

Years ago, I had a client who began working with me. She wanted to become a healer. She really wanted to make a difference in people's lives. But as we began to work together, she confessed that she was still smoking pot. Now, I don't have any problem with someone's choosing to smoke pot, but if you want to be attuned to the power of the universe, you cannot be dumbing down your senses. She herself acknowledged that smoking pot wasn't allowing her to utilize her mind in the strongest way possible. But she kept doing it. She was addicted to it. She felt that she just couldn't give it up. She was a slave to it.

She felt a simmering sense of discontent in her soul. But to graduate to the next level, she would have to give up smoking pot. She knew that in order to help others get free, she had to free herself.

You see, freedom isn't free. It requires you give up something so you can receive more.

During one of my visits to India, a man told me how they

catch monkeys. They put a banana in a cage in the middle of the town square. The monkeys see the banana and reach into the cage to grab it. But they can't get their hands out of the cage while they are holding the banana. They see someone coming to trap them. They could be free at any point. They could just drop the banana and run back to their tree. But they can't let go. They hold on to that banana and get captured.

What are you holding on to that is preventing you from running to freedom? Is it the outward appearance of success, even though it is killing you on the inside? Is it a habit that you can't seem to get over, even though you know there is more waiting for you if you can give it up?

What must you let go of to graduate to the next level?

Every moment is an invitation to choose to shed the layers and get more in touch with your soul.

When we think we are here simply to accomplish things, we get caught up in waiting for when we attain the goals we have in mind. Yet sometimes the journey that the goal takes you on, the journey that helps you become the highest version of yourself, is the greatest gift itself.

Every dream will take you on a journey. You might achieve it; you might not. But the real success is who you are becoming on that journey. The journey of life. There is no end goal. There is nowhere to get to. There is only NOW, HERE. When we acknowledge that we are really here for the evolution of our soul, every moment takes on meaning. Every moment is a test. Every moment is an invitation. Will I go back to the old way of doing things and have to learn the lesson again? Or will I choose the higher way and finally graduate?

Every moment, in some sense, is graduation day.

This is where all miracles happen.

When you stop trying to get somewhere else and embrace where you are now, you realize that this moment is the most important moment of your life.

CHAPTER | 6

THE MASTER ADDICTION

Real freedom is an inside job.

Real freedom isn't dependent on anything outside. No amount of money will set you free. No number of vacation days will set you free. All the information in the world can't set you free.

To be free, we must let go of our master addiction.

We've got to give up . . . control.

We live in the land of the free.

But the moment you take away our cell phone, our connection to the Internet, our wallet—the things we think we depend on—we collapse.

What kind of freedom is that? A freedom that is dependent on the external things of life.

Loosen Up

On the Liberation Experience, I remove everything that my clients may be holding on to for a sense of control.

From the moment they get dropped off at LAX, my clients do not know what we are doing, where we are going, when we are eating, where we are sleeping.

They are so used to being in charge of their lives. And to their lives being consumed by these details—accommodations, plans, itineraries, and schedules.

I take away their cell phone. They can't Google their way out of their situation.

I take away their money. They can't buy anything—food, a taxi ride, a plane ticket home.

I even make them give me their passport. They don't have photo ID.

I remove all the things they hold on to for a sense of freedom so that they can find out what remains. So they can access the true source of freedom within.

For the first few days, they resist the exact situation they've agreed to, asking in panicked voices, *Where are we going? When are we eating? What are we doing?*

And I never tell them. Ever.

Because they will finally realize there is no point. That there is nothing they can do. That they need to give it up.

That's when they finally surrender to the process that is the Liberation Experience.

Most journeys end at surrender. The Liberation Experience requires we begin with surrender. If we want to unravel the layers that have been keeping us trapped, surrender is not a luxury but a necessity.

You can afford to keep only what you are willing to surrender.

India is the best place to shed the layer of control. India exposes those parts of you that are gripping tightly to control. Why?

Because NOTHING goes according to plan in India. You can plan the most detailed itinerary, go over everything multiple times, reconfirm and double-check and memorize your checklist—and she will still chew you up and spit you out. The cabdriver won't show up or the hotel will suddenly be booked. There will be a festival blocking access to the town you thought you absolutely had to get to.

India is a great metaphor for life.

Because life doesn't tell you what's coming next. Life doesn't call you up one day and say, "Hi, this is life. In exactly two weeks, I will be sending a big crisis your way, so please get yourself ready."

Nope. Crises just show up unannounced. Life doesn't care what you have planned or that you might feel inconvenienced. BAM.

You are not in control.

You are not in control of when someone dies. Whether it rains. When you get sick.

We've got to learn to let go . . . and surrender our master addiction.

Control.

All of our coping mechanisms, all of the personas we've

constructed throughout our lives, stemmed from our need to control what was happening around us. *Oh, Mum and Dad aren't happy? Let me just try and change a bit to get the love I need. Oh, the world isn't accepting me? Let me just see what I can tweak about myself so that I start receiving attention and accolades.*

We try to control our past.

We try to control our future.

We try to control people.

But there is no freedom when we spend our lives doing this.

Ultimately, it's this addiction that creates all the suffering in our lives. We end up being controlled by the very thing we are trying to control.

Control Freak

When Arthur and I first got to India, I could feel from the moment we landed that he wanted to be in control. Every step we took, I sensed the questions in his mind: *Where are we going? Why are we going here? Should we really be doing this?*

He tried to hold them back, but eventually he would pester me. He asked me so many questions a day that I eventually stopped answering him.

I told him, "Arthur, life doesn't always tell you why something is happening at a given moment. Life doesn't tell you what is going to happen next. Life just happens. How you deal with life's ambiguity will determine the quality of your life and the experience you have every single moment. You can stand there demanding answers, stuck. Or you can trust life, take a step forward, and believe that the pieces of the puzzle will come together."

He looked at me like I was crazy.

Letting go of control is scary. I get it. If it weren't scary, we all would be walking around completely surrendered.

But I know that peeling back this layer is worth every amount of fear you will face.

On the third day of our journey, we were on our way to the caves of Ellora. We were sitting in the back of a beat-up cab, with a cabdriver who drove like a madman. If you want to give up control, take a cab ride in India. Cabdrivers don't obey traffic laws or speed limits. There are so many people on the streets that drivers learn to push ahead, throwing caution to the wind. When you sit in the backseat, watching your life flash before your eyes, it can be absolutely terrifying. You find your foot slamming an imaginary brake on the floor, wishing that you were in control.

But of course you are not. You are not in control. You just have to hold on to the sides of the car and pray!

Yes, India makes you pray. A lot.

There was no air-conditioning in the car, so we were sticking to the vinyl seats. When the driver was going fast, it was tolerable due to the breeze. But once we got to the outskirts of Aurangabad, we got stuck in traffic. So now we were hemmed in on all sides by other cars. There was no breeze. The only thing wafting in the windows was the stench of the garbage on the outskirts of the city.

Arthur had been quiet for most of the car ride, but finally he spoke up.

"Kute, have you gotten any messages from my family? I was hoping to hear something by now."

Being out of touch with his family was one of the most challenging parts of the process for him, and as we prepared for the trip, I said I would be checking messages intermittently. That if his family NEEDED to get in touch with him, they would be able to.

Well, it was now day three, and he hadn't gotten any messages. He was wondering how they were.

I turned to him and said, "There's nothing you need to know."

He did not like that answer.

He looked at me in confusion. "Kute, when did you call them? I mean, when could you have? There haven't been any opportunities."

"I find time when it is necessary. Listen, Arthur, just like you, I'm not in control of this journey. I'm not here to follow myself; I'm here to follow the journey. I'm not in control of India. I can make a plan or have an intention, but life has a way bigger intelligence and plan than I do. If you absolutely need to know every two days how your family is doing, I can't promise to give you that. So maybe you need to go home."

Arthur sighed in frustration and stared out the window. "Kute, you have to understand. I have seven children, and they need me. I just need to know how they are. It's not that complicated."

I took a deep breath. "Arthur, when you agreed to come on this trip, you said you were willing to trust the process. You said you were willing to trust me. Well, we're three days in, and you still don't trust it. You still don't trust me. You've got to trust me and trust this journey, or again, we both might as well go home."

He now turned to face me. We were like two cowboys at a showdown. Who would back down?

"Arthur, this journey is about learning to trust that life is handling everything. Do you feel, Arthur, that your kids and wife are dead?"

"No," he said honestly.

"Then why do you need to know?"

He shrugged his shoulders.

I knew we were at a crossroads. That it was trust me now or trust me never.

So I gave him a test.

"Okay, Arthur, if you want to stay here, if you want to continue the journey, then you have to show me you are ready. We are not going to the caves. Instead, we are going to shave your head."

His mouth dropped open.

"No way. I have a very important meeting a week after I get back and I'm not walking in there looking like a Martian. I'll do anything else to prove my commitment—go for another run, eat some crazy food—but I'm not going to shave my head! I just . . . I can't."

"But, Arthur, don't you see, it's not about shaving your head. If you won't shave your head, there will be many other things you won't be willing to do. You said you wanted the fullest experience of India, of the Liberation Experience, and now you aren't willing to shave your head? It's just one thing after another. *I need to check in with my family, I won't shave my head.* When are you going to give up and surrender?"

Now Arthur was yelling. The cabdriver looked back at us with concern.

"Seriously, Kute, it is an important meeting. They already think I'm strange enough at work without walking in there with a shaved head."

"Oh, so it's just about looking good, then?" I responded.

"Well, how exactly would I explain my shaved head? Listen, I did a seminar a couple of years ago where the leader wanted everyone to shave their head, and I didn't do it then. It didn't feel right. I just don't believe in it, Kute."

It was fascinating to watch him squirm and grasp for any semblance of control.

I chuckled. "You don't *believe* in it? What is there to believe in? This is not a religion; it's simply shaving your head. What is there to believe or not believe? If you really aren't willing to shave your head, we can't move forward, because there are many other things I'm going to ask you to do that won't make sense. And if you need to make sense of everything from this point on, it's just going to slow the process down."

I paused.

"You need to ask yourself this: Do you really want to transform? Perhaps, Arthur, you have reached your limit in terms of how far you are willing to go. You need to be honest with yourself about where you are at, rather than keep telling yourself that you want to transform."

We sat there in an eternity of silence while the sounds of India resounded outside the cab.

I continued: "Perhaps your destiny is that you are meant to go home. Arthur, I'm willing to surrender to that. But what I won't do is compromise the fullest experience. If I do, you'll go through these fourteen days and have a nice experience of India, but nothing will really be different. You'll still be fundamentally the same person. So we need to make a decision. We can stay and really do this—and that's going to involve you surrendering—or you can go home. Either way is fine. It is your call."

We sat in silence again. Arthur's head was in his hands. His shoulders were slumped forward and I couldn't see his face anymore.

Finally, he spoke up. "Kute, you're right. This thing I'm doing right now, I've been doing it my whole life. Resisting life, resisting change, shutting down, needing to control every single thing."

He paused.

"If I shave my head, do you think the hair will really grow back?"

I laughed and said, "Absolutely. That's just the way hair works. Unless you are going bald, it will grow back!"

"Okay, then," he said. "Let's do it."

In that moment, he surrendered.

He surrendered what he thought he wanted. He surrendered how he would look. He surrendered the master addiction, control.

And so I said with a smile, "Okay, Arthur, you don't have to do it."

He looked at me with his mouth agape. "What?"

"You don't have to shave your head! I don't really care whether you shave your head or not, Arthur. Shaving your head is not going to bring you freedom. But surrendering, that is what matters. Now it is up to you whether we shave your head or not."

Finally he laughed. "Let's do it, man! Now I want to shave my head!"

"Cabdriver," I said, "take us to the closest barbershop!"

The Killer Belief

When I take away my client's passport, make him stay in shitty rooms and sleep in 104-degree heat at night, it's not about dealing with the noise, the smells, the food, the poverty. It's not about shaving the head. It's really about surrender. I take away all control, and the only way to make it through is to throw one's arms up in the air and say, "Okay, I give up. I surrender. I will not resist anymore."

We have been trained to believe that if everything went our

way, we would be happy. But you can have only so much control over life. Attempting to control life will just keep us stuck, living small, cramped, limited lives.

So where are you a control freak? Where in your life do you find yourself frustrated when people or situations don't go the way you want? This is usually a sign that we are desperately clinging to the illusion of control. Because in our clinging to control, in our ideas about what SHOULD happen, lies the root of suffering.

But you don't have to go to India to shed this layer. Every day we have an opportunity. To cling to our desperate need to control or to open up to the endless possibilities of life.

Most of us take for granted that there will be times in life when we suffer.

But suffering is not necessary.

I know, I know. The Buddha said, "Life is suffering," but I believe it doesn't have to be.

Forgive me for saying so, but the Buddha didn't complete his sentence.

Life is suffering . . . when you resist it.

Suffering arises from the story that you add to the inevitable pain of life.

Suffering stems from the story you spin in your mind about what is happening.

I'm not saying life is all butterflies and rainbows. Whether you are a businessman or a Buddha, in this life, you will experience pain.

Pain is simply what happens in life. It cannot be avoided.

But suffering is optional.

If you're suffering, it's a choice.

It's a choice to believe that you are facing what I call the gap. The gap falls between:

Where I should be and *Where I am*

Or

How things should be and *How they are*

This is the gap. It doesn't matter whether the gap is big or small, increasing or decreasing. The fact that the gap exists causes us to suffer.

Where do you find yourself facing a gap?

Do you find yourself saying, *I should be . . . married, pregnant, rich, living in a bigger house, traveling the world?* It doesn't matter what those goals are. What matters is that we expect we should be somewhere, and when we aren't, we suffer.

When people first get to India, they often fight the reality that is. *It shouldn't be so hot. It shouldn't be so crowded. There shouldn't be so much poverty!*

We think things should be a certain way. And we try so desperately to get them to fit into the shape of our expectations.

When you let go of your attachment to your expectations, you can stop suffering.

That's right. When you let go of the idea of *how things should be*, you can stop suffering. Right now. You can put suffering in retirement!

So if you are suffering, stop and take a look at your thoughts. There is likely one line of thinking going through your mind.

I call this the Killer Belief. This belief is at the root of suffering.

The experience I'm having is not the experience I should be having.

I shouldn't be stuck in traffic.
He shouldn't have broken up with me.
They shouldn't have fired me!
I shouldn't feel this way.

Embedded in every one of those thoughts lies the belief: The experience I'm having is not the experience I should be having.

There are two things at play in the Killer Belief: First, resistance. You are resisting reality. And second, you are attached to the idea that YOU KNOW BEST. That what you can conceive of in your mind is more important than what is happening in life itself.

Your resistance to a situation doesn't change it. It just creates more suffering.

Think of Arthur. He wanted to be in control. He wanted to be able to talk to his family.

But was he in control?

No. He'd come to India, agreeing that he would trust me to make all the decisions.

If he'd stopped resisting and started accepting the truth, which was that HE WASN'T IN CONTROL, he would have stopped suffering immediately.

He could have stopped suffering IMMEDIATELY.

His resistance was what was causing his suffering. It wasn't the fact that he didn't know how his family was. His family was fine. He knew deep down that his family was fine.

But he wanted to be in control.

He was resisting reality.

Now, you can resist reality all you want, but it just keeps you stuck, disempowered, and resourceless. Being in a state of resistance is like going up to a brick wall and banging your head repeatedly against it, saying, "This wall shouldn't be here!"

Maybe not. You may even be right.

But it is there.

It is what is.

When you stop resisting, you open up to breaking the addiction. You discover the power of . . . acceptance.

Life Is Like a Box of . . . Mangoes

The first time I visited India, I didn't quite see its splendor. As I wandered India's cities and streets, instead of seeing her beauty, I saw only her flaws. *There shouldn't be animals in the street! How can they breathe through all this smog?* Needless to say, I hated India.

And then I visited the Taj Mahal. And after seeing the majestic beauty of this towering creation, after walking through its pristine hallways and its cool white rooms, I walked out into the overpowering India heat, and I just couldn't take it anymore. I was fed up with India. I had just walked through one of the most beautiful buildings in the world, a building that took twenty years to make and cost almost a billion dollars, and now I am walking out onto the streets where people lives off less than a dollar a day. It shouldn't be this way!

I walked to the train station, only to discover that my train was delayed and no one knew when it was coming.

Now that thought was added to my mantra. *The train shouldn't be late! Why can't anything run on time in this country!*

I didn't feel like being in India anymore.

Hours passed and nothing changed.

Until out of the corner of my eye I saw a beggar sitting on a bench.

He had no hands, only stumps. And in between his stumps, he held a mango. I soon noticed that he was completely fixated on eating this mango. It was as though nothing else in the world existed. It was like he was worshiping it, making love to this mango. Because he had no hands, it was not easy to eat the mango. It would slip from his stumps and he would have to wrestle with it to get it back in his grips just to eat it. But he was in a state of total bliss as he ate that mango.

It took him more than an hour to eat the fruit. I know because I did nothing else but watch him eat it. So when he was done, I walked over to him and asked, "How was it?"

"That was the best mango I've ever eaten," he said with a smile. And we both started to laugh!

"I've been watching you eat that mango for the last hour," I said.

"I enjoyed every bite of this mango," he insisted in broken English. "Life is like a mango. It's juicy. And it's messy. You can't eat a mango and really enjoy it without getting a little messy. You must accept it and enjoy it anyway."

I smiled at him. He was right. He was so right.

I was suffering because I was resisting India.

It was only when I stopped fighting what is and accepted India exactly as she is that she began to reveal her magic to me.

India is a lesson in duality. In America, the rich and poor tend to be separated. In India, even the richest man walks out his front door and is confronted with poverty. That's some of what makes India so intense. She is both so incredibly holy and beautiful and at the same time so wretched and ugly. She is filled with so much energy and life and color, and yet sickness and death confront you on every corner.

As I traveled throughout India, I would meet people who were just completely at peace with everything around them. At peace with the poverty. At peace with the orphans. At peace with what life is.

I began to realize that I had been looking for peace, looking for perfection in the world. India forced me to make peace with the duality of life, to come into a harmonious relationship with what is.

You can't truly be free until you make peace with the reality of life.

Life will always be filled with ups and downs. It's the law of nature. Yin and yang, light and dark. It's the nature of life and it's okay. We must embrace the duality inherent within life. Without night, there is no day. Without male, there is no female. Without black, there is no white. Without negative, there is no positive. Spending your life trying to make everything be light only creates suffering. Spending your energy to only hold on to light is not freedom. We must learn to embrace the darkness, and in doing so, we transform ourselves. In accepting the nature of life, we accept what is and what isn't and experience freedom. Life will always have expansion and contraction. When you stop seeking for perfection outside in the constantly changing world and realize that inside you is the ultimate perfection, that your soul is perfect beyond duality, beyond good or bad—when you understand that, you are free. Truly free. You see that life is perfect even in its seeming imperfection.

Peace is an inside job.

Don't look for peace in the world because you won't find it. When you connect with your true self you will have peace, even in the midst of chaos.

To accept that a mango is messy is to accept the reality of the situation.

To accept the reality of the situation is to bring you into relationship with your experience *as it is*. Not as what it should be. Not as what it could be.

What it is.

It's from this space that you have the power to change it rather than fight it.

Just think about all of the energy you put into fighting a certain experience. For example, I live in Los Angeles, and every day from about five to seven p.m., the infamous 405 Freeway is worse than a parking lot. Now, for an impatient person like me, this is my idea of hell! I know people who drive the freeway every single day on their way to and from work. And every single day on their drive home, they throw a fit! They shout obscenities. Cuss out other drivers. Cut people off. But their tantrum never makes the traffic move any quicker. It doesn't get them home any sooner or unplug stopped lanes.

Simply put . . .

Reality doesn't care.

It is what it is.

Your acceptance is the first step to freedom.

Now, some people may think that acceptance is weak. It is passive. It means you sit in an ashram saying, *There's nothing I can do.*

No. Acceptance is the most powerful thing in the world.

Because when you accept something as it is, you open up to the possibility that there might be a better way trying to emerge.

Acceptance allows you to look for the intelligence of the universe at work.

When you tap into the power of acceptance, it allows you to say, *Maybe what I* thought *was best isn't the best. Maybe there is something greater about to happen.*

It allows you to consider:

What if not getting what I thought I wanted in my life was a great gift from the universe?

I once heard a story about a king in Africa who had a childhood friend who responded to every situation in his life, whether positive or negative, with these three words: "This is good." One day the king and his friend were out on a hunting expedition. The friend would load and prepare the guns for the king. But on this day the friend did something wrong in preparing the gun. And after the king took the gun from his friend and fired it, the king's thumb was blown off! Looking at the situation, his friend replied as usual, "This is good."

"No! This is not good!" shouted the king, and he sent his friend to jail.

About a year later, the king was hunting in a forbidden area. Cannibals captured the king and took him to their village. They tied him to a stake and stacked wood around him in preparation to roast him for dinner. But as they went to start the fire, they noticed the king was missing a thumb. Being superstitious, the cannibals never ate anyone who was less than whole. So they untied him and sent him on his way.

When the king arrived miraculously back home, safe and sound, he remembered the event in which he lost his finger. He immediately went to the jail to find his friend.

"You were right!" said the king to his friend. "It was good that my thumb was blown off!" And with that, he told his friend the story. "I'm so sorry I sent you to jail," sobbed the king. "It was bad for me to do that!"

"No!" his friend replied. "This is good!"

"What do you mean?" asked the king, dumbfounded. "How could it be good that I sent my friend to jail for more than a year?"

"If I had not been in jail," said the friend, "I would have been hunting with you, and they would have eaten me!"

That is the power of acceptance.

So take a note from the man in the story and begin to see each situation in your life through the lens of *This is good.*

When you look back over your life, you will find that there are many moments that once looked bleak and disastrous, but from where you are today, were instead secret gifts.

Just try it. Try to remember a moment or situation that you considered at the time a complete disaster. Looking back, can you see how that "disaster" needed to happen so that you could have a different and better experience today?

Maybe it was a divorce that was devastating at the time but prompted you to deal with some ways you were holding yourself back in your life. Or perhaps a job opportunity you had counted on didn't come through, so instead you got the job you now have, which is where you met your husband.

If you hadn't "failed," you never would have met him.

I have learned through the ups and downs and wins and losses in my life that sometimes NOT getting what you thought you wanted in life—the job, the relationship, the house, the gig—is a great blessing from the universe.

Because the next part of overcoming suffering, of giving up the master addiction, is acknowledging: *There is something greater at work. There is something bigger than me that is seeking to work its magic.*

When we stop resisting life, when we can accept both what is and what isn't, it frees us up to access the next level of unpeeling. You discover within you a being that knows how to surrender, and you trust the unfolding of the beautiful mystery of life.

Blind Faith

At the heart of our resistance lies our distrust of the universe. We think we know best. We think we know what should be happening at each moment of life. We don't trust others. We don't trust that what is happening is what should be happening. We think we should be in control.

When I was young, my father would often ask me, "Son, did you bring yourself to this planet?"

"No," I would say.

"Then why worry so much?" he'd ask with a big belly laugh.

When you came into this world, you were well versed in

trust. You didn't have to go climbing around when it was time for your bottle. It was brought to you. When you pooped in your pants, you didn't judge, you didn't resist it, you just cried, and someone came and changed you. There was no striving for what you needed; there was just trust that it would come.

What would your life look like today if you could get back to that state? Trusting in the universe and surrendering to whatever is happening around you?

That kind of beautiful surrender is available to us all.

When you give up resistance, you discover the power of acceptance, and then you can start to truly trust that life will take care of you, has always been taking care of you. You have just always been in the way.

Once Arthur allowed me to shave his head, he was a new person. It was like a rite of passage he needed to go through before he could fully let go. Now that he had done the one thing he never thought he'd be able to do, the rest of the trip spread out before him full of possibility. He no longer clung to his need to hear from his family. He no longer asked five million questions a day. He was beginning to see how not being in control was actually an incredibly freeing experience.

But I knew that once we got back home, Arthur's tendency to control would come back. He wouldn't have anyone guiding him, so he'd feel the responsibility for all the choices that needed to be made.

It was time to show him that he could surrender, that he could trust. Not trust me, but trust life itself. Because that is the next step for my clients in India. They have finally begun to trust me as their guide. But I will not always be with them. Now they have to realize that life has been their guide all along. They just refused to listen.

Arthur and I were walking through the windy streets of Varanasi. After about an hour of just strolling through the streets, taking in our surroundings, I stopped Arthur.

"Okay, Arthur," I said. "It's time."

"Time for what?" he asked.

I held up a blindfold. "You are going to go on a blind trust walk. I am going to give you instructions about where to go and what to do. You are going to imagine my voice is the voice of the universe, and your role is simply to imagine that this is a metaphor for you living your life. Your only instruction is to follow the voice of the universe in this exercise. That is all you have to do."

He looked at me. And said, "Okay."

He leaned over so I could tie the blindfold around his eyes. He then turned around. I stood just a few feet behind him.

"I want you to feel with different senses now that you can no longer see. Feel around you. You can't see with your eyes or fall back on your mind or intellect. Instead, feel with your heart. Feel through your body. Are you ready to begin?"

He nodded.

"Begin to walk," I said.

He began to slowly walk forward, one step in front of the other.

"Turn left," I instructed.

He turned left. And paused.

"Now take two steps forward."

He did.

"Now, if you take another step forward you are going to step into a pile of cow shit. Step to the right." He did. "Arthur, how many times in your life have you heard the voice say, *If you take a step forward, you are going to step into a pile of cow shit in your business!* And how many times have you not listened to that voice?"

He nodded.

"Arthur, the universe has been speaking to you throughout your entire life. It speaks to you through your children; it speaks to you through your intuition; it speaks to you through your wife, your own inner voice. The problem is, you haven't listened. Keep walking. Five steps forward."

He obeyed.

"Your only role in your life is to simply listen. If you don't listen, you will step into a pile of shit . . . in your life. In order to really do this exercise, you must let go of trying to control the situation and instead simply listen. Then act, listen and act."

I kept giving him instructions. "Take one step forward, take another step forward. Stop. Turn left. Take another step forward. Turn around. Stop. Now I want you to imagine that the universe has a mission for you to do. Even though you don't know how you are going to do it, the universe is going to guide you."

I positioned him in front of a steep set of steps. I then had him take one step up. Followed by another one. Then another.

He would trip and lose his balance, as the steps were steep and uneven.

"Become totally present in this moment. Take another step, another step, another step." I kept guiding him.

Now, in the middle of the steps, I stopped talking. I was silent for about five minutes. Eventually Arthur turned his head. Then he said quietly, "Are you there? Kute, are you still there?"

And I said, as the universe, "I'm always here.

"I've always been here for you your entire life. Even when you haven't acknowledged me, even when you thought I wasn't here, I have always been here, guiding you all along."

Arthur smiled and tears began to stream down his face. We made it to the top of the staircase. I took off his blindfold. And we hugged.

When you surrender, you tap into a power greater than your mind, greater than your plans, greater than your ability to comprehend. When you stop trying to control, you are able to tune in to your consciousness.

You tap into life.

You don't have to drive life. You just have to take your foot off the brake.

When you do that, you go beyond the mind, you transcend limited logic.

You enter the miracle zone. It's a realm of unlimited possibilities. Where two plus two no longer has to equal four but equals whatever is necessary for the fulfillment of your destiny. Where a few fishes and loaves of bread can feed a crowd of thousands. Where a simple hunger strike can take down powerful governments.

Can you dare to access the miracle zone?

When you access the miracle zone, beautiful, mysterious things are bound to happen.

It is when you let go of control that your life can become so much bigger than you ever planned. Life is such a beautiful, amazing mystery! So many things have happened in our lives that we could never have planned. That we could never have figured out.

When I look back on my life, the best things that have happened to me are things that I never could have planned.

The green card. The $10,000 gift from God. The richest man in the world.

Could you believe? Could you let go of trying to make it all happen and just surrender to the miracles unfolding around you?

Give It Up

Your job is not to make things happen in your life. It's as if you went to the ocean and said, *I'm going to make the waves happen, I'm going to think hard enough to make the waves lap against the shore*. That would be ridiculous. The waves are already happening. The waves are crashing like clockwork. There is nothing you can do to stop or start them.

Are you willing to trust bigger than yourself?

You can live your own little life as "you" or you can surrender to the source of who you really are—your soul. It is in that realm that real greatness, magic, and miracles happen. This is the Gandhi zone, the Jesus zone. It's a level of consciousness that the miracle makers of our world are living in. When Michael Jordan plays, he is in the zone. He is not there. He has dissolved and the game is being played through him. He isn't in his head, his mind, thinking about how he is pivoting on his foot and how he is flicking his wrist. He is gone; he is being played by the game.

Or think of the other MJ, Michael Jackson. When you saw him in "real" life, he was this timid, self-conscious guy. But when he went onstage and began to perform, he was SOMETHING ELSE. MJ wasn't dancing; music and life and dance were happening through him.

When you surrender, that is when the big magic happens.

What is the definition of a good kiss? You completely let

go. You aren't thinking about what to do next, where to put your lips, how to tilt your head. You get wrapped up in the kiss itself, so much that you dissolve; you totally surrender. It is just happening through you.

What if we could live life that way?

Living in a state where you are always alert to what may be seeking to happen through you, instead of asking why things aren't happening. A state where you have let go of the way things should happen and stand openhandedly ready to receive whatever is coming.

If you can view your life as your masterpiece and you are the artist, you must recognize that it is time to peel back the layer of control. And access the power of surrender. True art does not stem from careful planning, from a death grip on control. A true artist holds the paintbrush lightly, ready and waiting for inspiration to come. It cannot be forced. It cannot be controlled. It can be given only when you surrender to the next level.

What Life can do through you is way more powerful than anything you can do on your own. Let go of the control you think you have and watch miracles unfold.

CHAPTER | 7

TODAY IS A GOOD DAY TO DIE

No one escapes death.

Not you. Not Gandhi. Not Jesus. Not Martin Luther King, Jr. Not Steve Jobs. Not Nelson Mandela. Not Ramana Maharishi.

Let me repeat, NO ONE.

We start dying the moment we come out of our mother's womb. That we'll go to a university, join the basketball team, get married, be happy, have nice parents, make a million bucks—none of that is guaranteed. The fact that we will die, that is guaranteed, yet somehow we run from it. We avoid it. We suppress it.

We do all sorts of things to pretend it's not going to happen.

We've got to stop lying to ourselves.

It's time to look death in the eye.

Rocky Mountain High

When I was twenty-three years old, I almost died on top of a mountain.

It wasn't how I'd envisioned my first trip to India panning out.

As I traveled first through Mumbai and then through some of the smaller towns throughout India, I took everything in. I felt like my heart was getting ready for something. I thought maybe I'd meet a guru who would give me all the answers to life's problems, or I'd meditate in some hidden cave and come close to enlightenment.

Instead, I found myself vomiting in the Himalayas.

This was not my idea of enlightenment!

It happened on my way to the source of the Ganges River. The source of the Ganges is a hugely popular pilgrimage destination. Hindus believe that bathing at the source of the river washes away all your sins. But the trip is far from easy. The Ganges originates in the slow trickle of melting ice from the glaciers at the top of the Himalayas. At 14,000 feet above sea level.

Many pilgrims begin their journey in Gangotri, a town at the base of the Himalayas. The hike from Gangotri to the source is roughly twelve miles. But it is straight up the mountain.

Now, I consider myself in pretty good shape. So a hike of twelve miles wasn't daunting. I'd hiked the entire Camino. This wasn't going to be a big deal.

After spending a night in a hostel, I headed out the next

morning around six-thirty, the air bracingly cold despite the sun burning bright in the sky. I carried a small backpack and nothing else. I figured it would take me about five to six hours to reach the source.

But I'd felt a bit off as soon as I'd woken up. My stomach was churning and I felt slightly nauseous. Like a good spiritual pilgrim, I convinced myself that it was due to the energies of the Himalayas. I pressed on, accepting the uncomfortable feelings, but praying they would pass.

As I began to hike, the feeling intensified. *This isn't good,* I thought. I kept thinking of the stories you hear of people getting sick in India, from food or water or illnesses like malaria.

Was I crazy to keep going? What did I think I would find at the top of this mountain, God himself?

Here I was, in the stunning beauty of these snowcapped mountains, a place where I'd always dreamed I'd be, and I could barely walk because of my stomach.

Soon I began to get sick. Every thirty minutes, I would vomit on the side of the path. Then it was diarrhea. Every time I was sure the purging had to be over, there was more purging.

Holy men were running up the mountain barefoot, passing me in a seeming state of blissfulness.

And I felt as if I was in hell.

But I knew it would take me a couple of hours to get back to Gangotri if I turned around. I prayed the source wasn't much farther. I couldn't imagine coming to India and not making it to the source of the Ganges.

So I kept going.

Walk. Shit. Cry. Walk. Vomit. Cry.

Repeat.

Finally I had experienced four hours of intense sickness. I felt like I had nothing left in me to purge. I lay by the side of the path. My eyes closed. With hardly enough energy to get up.

This was it.

I was going to die.

Okay, God, I'll see you soon.

No, it wasn't quite that easy.

I'd always wondered how I would handle the moment I came face-to-face with death. But here I was, too exhausted even to be afraid! I felt this acceptance pass over me, a deep level of surrender that I hadn't experienced before. *Okay, I can't make myself any better here. I can't drag myself to a hospital. This is where it ends for me.*

Death is the ultimate surrender.

Was I sad that it was ending so soon? At twenty-three?

Yes, sure, I was beyond sad. Tears were streaming down my face.

But I was helpless. I was alone. There was nothing I could do up here. There was nothing else to do but to let it go. There was nothing else to do but surrender it all. My dreams, my family, my life.

Death has a way of making you think about life honestly. It cuts through all the lies and pretense. So I thought about the people I knew I had hurt in my lifetime and tried to make mental amends. I said goodbye to my mother and father and hoped they would feel some peace that I had died here, in India, in a place I had always dreamed of visiting. I thanked God for the beautiful life that I had lived.

But I kept thinking . . . how much farther to the source?

If I have to die somewhere, why not right where it is said it all begins?

So I pulled myself up. And kept going.

Finally, after ten hours of hobbling and shitting and vomiting, I looked up and realized that somehow I had made it. I had arrived at the source. Just in time to die.

I threw myself on the banks of the small, trickling stream. I plunged my hand in the water and splashed my face. It was the coldest cold I'd ever felt. And with that water, awakening me, cleansing me, I felt ready. I just had to go find a place. A place to lie down and die.

There was a large tentlike structure off to the side, built by the sadhus and holy men for pilgrims to sleep in after their summit. I crawled inside, found a space to lie down, and collapsed on the floor.

It was now late afternoon, the shadows long, the cold coming in. The day was done. As was I.

I had given it all up. This was it. This was where my life was ending.

I fell asleep expecting that blackness to be the end of my life.

And then I opened my eyes.

I saw the ceiling of the tent. I felt the hard ground under my still-aching body. Shit. This isn't heaven.

Wait, is this hell?

I pulled myself out of the tent.

Stared up at the bright blue sky.

Then I laughed out loud.

I was still alive.

But I wasn't the same.

Newborn Walking

I woke up on that mountain a different man.

I woke up no longer afraid of the moment my life will end.

When your fear of death evaporates, your fear of life evaporates.

Before coming to India, I had never really thought much about death. Sure, I knew it was something that happened to all of us. Sure, perhaps I wondered how I would face it when it came. But I'd never before felt deep in my bones . . . ticktock, ticktock. Boom! Your time is up.

Now something felt different inside me. Like I suddenly had more space in what was previously a tiny room. The size of the room had expanded. I had expanded.

I was still nauseous. I was still exhausted. I still had to get down the mountain. But I wasn't worried about how it would happen. It just didn't matter.

Once you've accepted death, what is there to be afraid of?

You hear about people who come back from a life-altering accident profoundly transformed, so much so that they wouldn't change anything about the accident. Despite losing limbs or the ability to walk, people know that the perspective they gained from facing death is worth more than a perfect body, more than their mobility, more than a "normal" life.

When you sit in the darkness, expecting that your time on earth has come to an end, and then you wake up with another day? You get reborn.

That morning, standing as close to the sun as I'd ever been, I knew I had been given another chance at life. I was no longer afraid of what might happen. It's like the worst had already happened . . . and I was still here! Now I was just excited about the possibility of what COULD happen next.

I begged one of the Sherpas on the trail to let me use his donkey to carry me down the mountain. He saw the state I was in and relented. And clinging to the back of a donkey teetering on the edge of the mountain, I made it down to Gangotri. Where I learned that I had had a very bad case of . . . altitude sickness.

I had to laugh again. Altitude sickness had just given me one of the greatest lessons of my life.

Facing death frees us to live this thing called life boldly, with nothing to lose.

Stop Eating Seeds in Your Cage

I once heard a fable of a traveler from India who went to Africa to buy some local products. And while in the jungle, he saw thousands of beautiful parrots that could talk. He decided to capture one and take it home as a pet. Back in India, he kept his parrot in a cage and fed him seeds. He played music to him every day. He figured the bird had a pleasant existence.

A couple of years later, when he decided to go back to Africa, he asked his parrot if there was any message he could deliver to his parrot friends back in the jungle.

"Tell my parrot friends that I am very happy in my cage. I am enjoying each day and I send my love," said the parrot.

When the man arrived back in the jungle in Africa where he'd captured his pet, he shared his parrot's words with the other birds dwelling there. Just as he finished his story, the eyes of one of the parrots filled with tears and he fell over dead. This alarmed the man. He decided that the parrot must have been very close to his pet, and this was probably the reason for his demise.

When the traveler returned home, he told his pet what had happened. As he finished the story, his pet parrot's eyes filled with tears and he fell over and died in his cage. The man was astounded and figured that his pet parrot had died from hearing about the death of his friend. So the man carefully gathered up his beloved pet's body and carried it out to the trash. As soon as he laid its body in the garbage can, the parrot fluttered his wings and flew up to a branch on a nearby tree.

"Wait! You're not dead after all!" shouted the man. "You tricked me! Why did you do that?"

"Because," said the parrot, "the bird back in Africa sent me a very important message."

"What was the message?" the man asked.

"He told me that if you want to escape from your cage, you must die while you're alive."

Die while you are alive, and you break open the door to your cage.

Are you willing to die?

I mean, are you really ready and willing to die?

This is the question I ask my clients before inviting them to join me on the Liberation Experience.

There is no Liberation Experience unless you are willing to leave and never come back.

To help them process whether they are ready, I require my client to create a last will and testament. I tell them, "Get your affairs in order. Who gets your money? Your car? Who will take over your business? Who gets your crazy senile cat?"

Did you know that the majority of adults under the age of thirty-four do not have a will? To create your will means you face the reality of death.

Instead, we love to pretend we are immortal. We cling to the things and relationships that we accumulate in this life as if they are ours, things that we will have claim to forever.

But ultimately we can't take any of it with us.

So take the time to write your will. Think about what happens when you are no longer here. Let go of those possessions and imagine them having a good life after you are no longer here. Think about those you love and what they may need without you in this life.

I'm not suggesting that it's time to donate all your things or dissolve all your relationships. But when you accept the fact that your life in this body is temporary, your relationships take on new meaning. They become more precious.

They become gifts instead of so-called guarantees.

I have my clients write goodbye letters to their families. Kids, spouses, parents, siblings. They write letters expressing all that is left unsaid. Imagining what they would want loved ones to know in case they don't come back from India. They don't mail the letters. I hold on to them. I carry them with me our entire time in India. I promise my clients that if something happens to them, I will mail the letters. But I want my clients to be ready. I want them to face the inescapable truth of their mortality.

Are You Ready?

I have only had one client who was scheduled to go on the Liberation Experience and ultimately couldn't face his death.

We had been planning the trip for months. But I could tell, as the departure date approached, that he wasn't doing his homework. He would avoid meetings with me and miss deadlines. So I called him on the Friday night before we were supposed to leave. Our flight to India was on Sunday.

I asked him what was going on.

He was full of excuses. "Kute, I'm really sorry, man, but I don't think I can do this. I've got these investor meetings that are coming up and my company really needs me here to attend them. I just . . . I mean . . . I didn't know when we first started talking that this deal would come up, so . . . I just . . . I just don't know, man."

"Sure, sure, there's a lot going on. I hear you. But you know what the real problem is. Those excuses are BS. I'm sorry, man, the truth is you're afraid."

There was silence on the phone.

I wasn't going to say anything. He had to know that this was the truth. Investor meetings? I mean, there will always be more meetings to go to.

Do you want to make a deal or do you want to reclaim your life?

And then I heard him begin to cry.

"Kute, you are right. I'm terrified. Kute, I can't die! I've got a wife and kids. They need me! I can't abandon them. Please, just tell me I'm going to be okay, that everything's going to be fine and I'll come back fine, and I'll go. Then I'll go, I promise."

I sighed and smiled. "I can't tell you that. If I did, I'd be pacifying you, sure, but it would be a lie. None of us know.

There are no guarantees in life. I don't know what will happen. I can't guarantee that you will be fine."

I paused.

"Go on this journey only if you are ready. Are you ready?"

He promised he would think it over and call me back the next night.

At ten p.m. on Saturday night, my phone rang.

"I can't do it. I can't go. I'm sorry."

I told him that it was okay, I understood, but at this late date, there were no refunds. Not to mention the biggest cost—his soul.

Was he really sure?

"No, I'm not ready. I can't go."

He is the only Liberation Experience client I have ever had who was hours away from being set free who couldn't do it. Who couldn't face the reality that one day he would die and that he had no control over when that would happen. Instead, he decided to stay trapped in his cage, eating seeds, when a delicious feast of freedom awaited him.

Burn It Up

When I take clients to India, I make them face their death.

They see just how fragile this life can be.

We go to Varanasi. Varanasi is said to be the holiest city in the world, sitting on the banks of the Ganges River. Hindus believe that if you have your ashes thrown into the Ganges in Varanasi, you escape the cycle of death and rebirth and go to heaven for an eternity. So thousands of families come every year, traveling hundreds of miles, to lay their loved ones to rest here, in hopes of setting their souls free.

I took Carlos there, but I didn't tell him any of this. He had no idea where we were going or why. When we got off the train, I had Carlos follow me through the winding streets and narrow alleyways as we tripped over cobblestones and wound our way through the kids, cows, shopkeepers, and beggars who made passage nearly impossible. The scent of incense permeated the air, and we began to follow that scent down to the river.

Soon we began to hear chanting.

I turned to look. And as I did, the crowds of people filling the streets all stopped what they were doing, moved to the side, and respectfully created a pathway for the large procession of people weaving through the streets, chanting and carrying a stretcher.

On the stretcher was a body.

Then, as if someone had hit a pause button, the streets fell silent and still as we waited for them to pass us by.

And then somebody hit start. Life continued. The noises swelled as if nothing had happened; kids began playing, beggars begging, cowbells clanging.

We followed this family down to the banks of the river.

And stopped and stared.

We had arrived at a burning ghat, where the priests performed cremations.

Ten feet away from us, a priest was circling through piles of wood. On the piles were dead bodies. The priest was throwing sandalwood powder on the bodies, and one by one, lighting the piles of wood as he offered last rites.

Carlos stood beside me with fear in his eyes. I nodded and stepped back.

The priest began to prepare another pile of wood for the body that had just arrived.

The family stood on the bank, crying and singing and chanting. They were here to say goodbye to their loved one. To watch his body burn. But ultimately, they were there to watch his soul set free when his ashes were thrown into the river.

Because they knew their loved one was no longer contained in that body.

Transfixed, Carlos and I sat down. And watched body after body burn into ash.

Do you know that it takes about two hours for a human body to dissolve inside a fire? I know that because we watched it. We watched the head burn, the neck dissolve; we heard the flesh sizzle, the bones collapse. Until every single bone and organ and sinew disappeared. In the end there was nothing but ash.

Nothing but ash.

Now, it is one thing to intellectually know that we all die. It is quite another to stare it in the face, to watch a body transform from a solid form into ashes that literally blow away on the wind.

As the bodies finished burning, the ashes were thrown into

the Ganges. This was the moment their souls were set free. Cows grazed and walked all over the remaining ashes, which the wind picked up and blew through the air. We breathed the air into our lungs.

The air we were breathing was life-giving. And yet filled with death. It was the perfect cycle of life.

Carlos turned toward me in shock, his face covered with ash, tears streaming down his dirty face. "Why, Kute? Why did you make me watch that?"

"Well, Carlos, in case you're curious about what your life will end up as, no need to go to a psychic, just take a look at those bodies burning. That is the fate of all of us. If you can make peace with that, you'll be free, because you realize that you can't be just *this*," I said, pointing at my body. Carlos continued to stare out over the river.

"Our body is finite. One minute it is alive, moving, functioning, running, shitting, making money, making love. Then the next moment it's gone, thrown in the Ganges. Cows grazing on what's left on the ground, walking on it, shitting on it. So much for thinking that it's so incredibly important."

Carlos laughed through his tears, shaking his head.

"Think about it. If we were really our body, that family wouldn't have brought their father here to the banks of this river. If our body is who we are, our essence, they would have just propped that body up at the dinner table and continued life as if nothing was different. But they know that their father, who he *really* is, is no longer in that body. That's the part they love. That's the part that continues on. So there has to be something that lives and breathes in our body. What's living and breathing in you and me? What is that?"

Carlos shrugged his shoulders.

"No matter how famous you become, no matter how much money you make, no matter how great a physique you develop or how healthy or organic you eat, *there* is the end," I said, pointing at a burning body. "Take a good look. It's time to accept it, be done with it. So much of what we do in our lives is to try and avoid death, but if we are not the body, what is to fear? The body will change, decay, and break down. But what you are as pure soul is untouchable."

Carlos nodded and sank to his knees. Tears continued to course down his face.

"We are afraid to face death because we think we will cease to be when our heart stops beating in our chest. If we are our body, then when we die, we are gone. And that is a terrifying thought.

"But what is REAL can never be lost. And what is unreal can never last."

The breeze picked up and the smoke and ash blew straight into our faces.

"Carlos, you have been conditioned to believe that you are simply this body, this material flesh of skin and bones that your spirit inhabits for a very short period of time. When in fact the very essence of who you are is infinite. Beyond birth. Beyond death. *You* are what's real. The real you. Your spirit. Your body is what is unreal. It is temporary. Impermanent. Transitory."

I paused.

"You, Carlos, are not the body. You, Carlos, cannot die."

We sat there in silence for a few minutes, and then I asked him, "Carlos, are you ready?"

He looked up and said, "Yes."

And I motioned toward the river.

"That river represents all of humanity. That river is believed to cleanse your sins and send you to heaven. Go, and let your old life be washed away."

Carlos got up, went down to the water, and slowly walked in. Soon he was submerged there, swimming, floating, and releasing the old way of doing things.

When he came out, he was ready for the next lesson.

He had shed the layer.

He is not his body.

Just like you are not your body.

That you somehow think this sack of flesh and bones is YOU is an illusion that must be peeled away.

It's Just Fancy Packaging

We've been hypnotized to believe that we are our physical form. So life becomes an endless chase of beauty, health, youth.

And our culture loves that! Because the more we identify with the body, the more material things we can be sold. The perfect outfit, the best diet, the most revolutionary procedures—those don't mean anything unless we buy into the lie that we are the body.

But why do we care about a perfect body? If it is just the vehicle for our soul? If it is just something temporary, something we can't take with us?

When you overidentify with the body, it becomes a cage just as much as the birdcage the parrot died to escape.

I live in Los Angeles. The City of Angels is truly a wonderful and unique place. I'm proud to call it home. But the heart of Hollywood places so much focus on physical beauty, with our outer layer. There is so much pressure to be and look a certain way. Women everywhere, but especially women in LA, have been conditioned to believe *I am my body, I am my body, I am my body.* They are so tightly identified with their physical form that it becomes a source of paranoia. A weight gain of five pounds can be soul crushing. They are convinced that how they look on the outside is what will lead to success and happiness. Thus they spend countless hours and untold sums of money on Botox, plastic surgery, and extreme diets, just to try and perfect something that in the end will simply be burned up.

We are not the body. This is just our packaging. It is as fleeting as the wind.

There is nothing wrong with the body. Let me make this clear. The body is a beautiful manifestation of life itself. It's a work of art. It is a miracle.

But it is just the vessel for our soul.

When we get attached to the body and begin to associate with it as "me," we suffer.

Your body doesn't determine your worth or value.

What's important is your relationship with the body. Where you can honor it. Love it. Dwell in it. And at the same time not be attached to it.

What if you thought about your body as you do about your car? I mean, I love my car. I take care of my car. It takes me places. I don't know what I'd do without it. I love how I feel when I drive it. But it changes. It's going to get scratched. It's going to need a new transmission. I've got to switch out the tires every now and then.

I don't think I'm a failure when my car needs attention or starts to break down. I don't blame it, hate it, shame it.

I love it and give it the attention it needs. I realize that it has a life-span. It will not last me forever. It's here to do a job, for a while.

So can you stop? Despite the media's trying to brainwash you, can you let the body go? Respect it, love it, take care of it. But know the real you is so much more.

Your hair color? Your weight? Your wrinkles? Your tan?

They will all be burned up in the end.

They don't define you.

They do not encompass your worth.

What is within you that cannot die?

That is the true treasure.

The part of you beyond birth and death. The part of you who knows what is really important. The part of you who knows that . . .

YOU ARE THE ONE.

Teatime with Your Destiny

No matter how fast you can run, death is always going to be nipping at your heels.

It's time to turn around, face it, and embrace it.

You've got to make death your friend. Keep it close, not as some morbid thing, but as an inspiring reminder of the preciousness of each moment.

Invite death to tea. Sit with it. But whatever you do, don't run.

You can't outrun death.

As you sit with death, put on your favorite music. Wear your best outfit. Put your hand on its heart and gently whisper into its ear, "Thank you, dear friend, for reminding me to live."

Befriending death holds the power to change how you live immediately.

When my clients begin to do the prep work for the Liberation Experience, when they begin to pull together their wills and begin to write their letters, they are already transformed. Before they even get on the plane, their lives are altered.

You see, when you prepare for and accept your death, you no longer take every day for granted. You know that each day brings you one day closer to your death. So your relationships take on new meaning. Death demands you live with a fierce urgency of now. You realize you can't hold back about how you feel because you realize that if I don't come back *from India, from work today, from the grocery store,* I don't want to leave this unsaid. My clients open up to their spouses and their children. Their employees and coworkers. Walls come down. Conversations that have been percolating for years come to light.

Life begins to be truly, deeply, honestly . . . lived.

So.

What would you say if you knew that time was running out?

To your wife? Your son? Your mother? Your partner?

How would knowing that there was no tomorrow change the way you lived today?

Stop what you are doing. Put down the book. Go find a mirror. And say to yourself as you stare into your eyes: "I am going to die."

Say it again. "I am going to die."

Now look at your hand. Touch it. Poke it. Say out loud, *This thing will die.*

Close your eyes. Notice how your breath continues to move in and out through your nostrils. Without your doing anything. Stop and simply FEEL what is breathing you. Get curious about that. You can try and hold your breath, but ultimately life takes over and forces you to take another breath.

What is breathing you is a mighty force that cannot be destroyed. Feel your power. It's a power beyond the body alone. It is the force of your soul.

That force is who you really are.

That inner source is where we access true power. When you face the end up front, you are freed up to go about each day with all self-consciousness removed. With the willingness to risk big.

You become truly bold.

Today Is a Good Day to Die

So what if today was the last day of your life?

Would you be ready?

Would you be prepared to throw your arms wide open and say, *Take me—I'm ready? I've given everything?*

Or would there be some regret?

What's unexpressed?

What's unsaid?

There's no guarantee you will have tomorrow.

The only guarantee is this moment.

When death arrives, much of what you stressed about, worried about, fretted about, screamed about, argued about, gossiped about, cried about, fought about won't really matter. But you will care about the answers to these questions.

Did you love those in your life as fully as possible?
Did you experience life as deeply as possible?
Or did you stay trapped in your cage?

Years ago, I took one of my dearest friends, Sri, to Ghana to celebrate my birthday. Sri was from India and had always wanted to go to Ghana. While we were there, I was at the house of some friends and some people were drumming. I began to dance wildly to the beat. Now, I can't really dance, but I was just sort of flailing about, without a care in the world. Sri watched me from a distance with eyes full of longing. He came up to me afterward and said, "Kute, I wish I could dance like you. I have always been afraid. I just freeze up."

"What do you mean?" I laughed. "I can't dance. I just let the energy flow!"

"I wish I could do that!" he said.

"You can!" I said. "Let all of your judgments go and just go for it! Lose your mind," I told him.

The next day we went to see one of the great shamans of Ghana. And as the shaman began to spin as he went into a trance, Sri also stood up as if something had possessed him. And in front of the thousands of villagers that had gathered, Sri began to whirl around. As I watched, I could feel his soul breaking free of the shackles that his mind had been placing on him for years. It brought me to tears to watch him dance without a care in the world. He seemed so . . . free.

After this amazing day, I said goodbye to Sri to come back home, and he continued to travel through Ghana alone. One month later, I called Sri, but his daughter answered the phone. She told me he was in the hospital, but that she would pass on the message and he would surely call me tomorrow. She also told me that her father had had the time of his life in Ghana. "He just wanted me to tell you that he loves you" were her final words. The next day I called the hospital to check on him and received the message that my dearest friend had died. At first I didn't believe them. I couldn't believe that I had missed my chance to speak to him one last time. I put down the phone and sobbed, knowing that I would no longer be able to hug him, laugh with him, experience life with him.

A few days later, though, I sat thinking of our last time together on Earth. And all I could do was smile. To this day, when I think of my friend Sri, I do not cry that he is no longer here. Instead, I see that image of him dancing so freely without a care in the world, as if that day was his last, and he had finally dared.

He finally dared to dance while he was alive.

So I ask you . . .

Will you dance?

Will you dare to live boldly, knowing that you have faced death, but that who you are can't really die?

Can you step out of your cage and start living each day as if it was your last?

It might be. There are no guarantees.

It's time. Time to take your best dress out of the closet and wear it. Take your best plate out of the cupboard and use it. Take your best loving off the shelf and share it.

The time is now.

You are never born. You never die. The real you is infinite.

CHAPTER | 8

LOVE NOW

At the end of our lives, everything boils down to this:

Did you love fully?

Or did you spend your life holding back?

Living Buddhas

I learned the greatest lesson about life from a man named Dwarko-Ji. I met him in India, in the town of Bodhgaya. He was eighty years old at the time, the last living disciple of Gandhi.

For more than fifty years, Dwarko-Ji has been providing shelter and education for thousands of orphans all across India. He welcomes them into his orphanage, treating them as his own children. And he teaches them to live by Gandhi's principles of nonviolence in his orphanage, as well as in more than three hundred schools that he has created across India.

As if that wasn't enough, he also brings in top Indian eye

doctors for one of the largest free eye camps in the world, providing 50,000 locals with free eye operations.

Dwarko-Ji has been inspiring thousands by his life of service and his spirit of selflessness. Luminaries such as Martin Luther King and Marlon Brando have come to meet him. J. Krishnamurti met him and was deeply impacted by his presence. The Dalai Lama considers him a great friend and has even said, "I may teach compassion, but Dwarko-Ji lives it."

Yet there is almost nothing written about this man. He doesn't care about publicity. His work is in his orphanage, with his children. To him, this is all that matters.

On my first trip to India, I couldn't wait to meet this man. Dwarko-Ji invites outsiders to come and live in the orphanage, volunteering with the children and seeing what life is like in India. I arrived full of excitement and energy. I knew I could help these children and couldn't wait to see how they would respond to my presence.

But after two weeks, I was frustrated. After living on the streets, without parents or siblings, shelter or food, the children possessed few social skills. Many of these children are found living in trash heaps or running wild in the streets. They do not always respond to human kindness. They are still figuring out whether they can trust people.

No matter what I did, the children barely spoke to me. I tried a number of different things to try and connect with them. But nothing seemed to work.

Feeling defeated, I pulled Dwarko-Ji aside one morning.

"I'm sorry, Dwarko-Ji, but I am feeling discouraged. I

don't know if what I am doing is making any difference. I'm going to take a break and go to the Bodhi Tree and meditate for a few days."

Dwarko-Ji looked at me with eyes full of compassion. He nodded slowly and then said in his deep, gravelly voice, "It's beautiful that you go and meditate at the Bodhi Tree by the statue of the Buddha. But while you're meditating, just make sure your heart doesn't turn to stone sitting there. Because right here in this orphanage, in front of your very eyes, are living Buddhas just waiting to be worshiped."

I felt like someone had punched me in the stomach.

I stood looking at this wise man. I was twenty-three years old. I was still figuring out what life was all about.

Dwarko-Ji knew. He knew what life was about.

What is there to do but love now?

I thanked Dwarko-Ji for his wisdom, deeply humbled. He patted my hand with understanding. And I sat back down and I loved those children.

Going someplace to meditate wouldn't change anything. My meditation was right here. In this orphanage. Yes, I could go meditate and try and be inspired. Or I could realize that all the love I had to give was right inside me. It wasn't dependent on how these children acted or reacted. I had the power inside to love them . . . or not.

It is easy to love the saint. It is easy to love those you like. It is easy to love when life is going well.

The true spiritual practice is learning to love no matter what. Not when everything is perfect. Not when you FEEL like loving.

This is the layer that we must peel in order to access our soul.

We think there are certain conditions that must be met in order to feel love, in order to express love. But loving is not about something out there. It is only about what is in your heart. And in your heart is the endless capacity to love.

This is the path of Love Now.

True love does not originate outside of you. It is not something that can be deserved.

True love is always freely given, with nothing expected in return.

So will you love fully?

IF not, WHY not? What do you think needs to be different in order for you to love?

Whatever you may think, it is an illusion.

You can love fully right now.

Nothing is stopping you.

Nothing.

I Am a Child of Love Now

There are times that I am amazed it took me this long to learn this lesson. Because all along, right in front of my face, was a living lesson in loving now.

My parents.

I am living proof that loving someone doesn't have to be dependent on a certain set of characteristics or on the way they make you feel. That love is what stems from the calling of your heart.

When my father was eight, he began to have dreams in which a Japanese man would teach him about life and its mysteries. My father had no idea who this man was or why he kept appearing in his dreams, but this dream kept recurring throughout his life.

This dream continued into his adulthood. One day he walked into a bookstore and a book fell off the shelf in front of him. When he bent down to pick it up, he saw the face of the man who had been coming to him in his dreams all those years. He stared at the photo in shock. As he examined the book's cover, my father learned that the man was a well-known Japanese spiritual teacher who had millions of followers.

My father decided to write him and share how he had been seeing him in his dreams. The spiritual teacher was so touched that he sent his son-in-law to Ghana to meet my father.

After watching my father preach, the son-in-law invited my father to travel with this spiritual master on his upcoming lecture tour. My father agreed, and as the son-in-law prepared to return to Japan, my father made a simple request: "Please pray for me. I am searching for my wife."

Meanwhile, in Japan, my mother found herself unmarried at twenty-eight years old, ancient in her culture to be unwed. So she prayed. "I will marry anyone you tell me to marry. Just make it clear to me that it is my soulmate. Give me the knowing. I don't care what he does for a job, about his race, his age. I will surrender my heart if you show me he is the right one."

One evening my mother attended a lecture by the son-in-law of this Japanese guru. He announced that there was a "miracle man from Africa" who would be coming to speak to the congregation. Instantly, my mother got the chills! She heard a voice that said, "This is your husband."

The next day she asked her sister to help her write my father a letter. My mother didn't speak English, but her sister did. So slowly she dictated a letter to my father, saying how much everyone one in Japan was looking forward to his arrival.

Meanwhile, my father had traveled to London before going on to Japan to meet this spiritual guru. And while he was in deep meditation, he heard a voice say to him, "Your wife will come to you tomorrow!" The next day he found a packet of letters waiting for him. As he held my mother's envelope in his hands, they began to shake. He felt a deep knowing and said, "This is from my wife."

Once he read her letter, he immediately wrote back and introduced himself. And then, at the end of the letter, he wrote: "Would you be open to moving to Ghana?"

A week later he received her response.

"If it's God's will," she wrote back.

A few days letter, she received a letter back from him. "Yes, it's God's will," he wrote. "Marry me."

Without hesitation, my mother ran to find her sister. "Just write the word YES!" she said excitedly.

As my father prepared to go to Japan, he decided he wanted one more sign from the universe that this was the woman he was supposed to marry. So he asked for a vision of her and went out to have a dress made for her. If the dress fit, it would confirm that she was the one.

Once my father arrived in Japan, he and my mother met briefly and spent forty-five minutes alone. It was an interesting meeting during which they communicated only by way of hand gestures and pointing, as they had no common language. Finally my father opened the box that contained the dress he'd had made for her.

She went into another room to try it on.

And then walked out. It was a perfect fit.

A month later they were married and began their life in Ghana, and decades later they're still together!

Now, my parents' story may be more extreme than most, but you hear about arranged marriages around the world, where people who were strangers before they married ultimately come to share the deepest, truest love. It seems foreign to us, being from a culture that prioritizes attraction and chemistry and making sure we are "in love." But there is something there, in the seeds of my parents' story, that shows that love is not contingent on certain feelings or emotions.

Love is a commitment to share what is in your heart with another person, no matter who they are, what language they speak.

But most of us have been conditioned to hold back our love.

We go from being young children who say "I love you" to the dog on the street and the man behind the counter to adults who reserve their love for people they can trust, for people who earn their love, for people who love them back.

We are conditioned to believe that love is based on certain conditions. Get good grades, be a good girl, look a certain way. That our love is dependent on a certain set of actions. If someone doesn't measure up, love should be retracted.

We learn that our love should be held in reserve. It is for our family, our girlfriend, our children, our spouse. We cling to these people. They are the ones who get our love.

But we hold the power to love anyone in any moment.

Making Love to a Post

It was a few days before Jennifer was scheduled to leave India, but I knew we still had some work to do because she had so much trouble trusting anyone. She held back her love because of all the ways she had once been hurt. She didn't think it was safe to love.

Sure, she could continue to lock her love up inside. Or she could open her heart and dare to give it away. It didn't matter what the other person did. Whether anyone deserved it. What mattered was who she was. She was love. She would never be able to "find" herself until she reopened her heart.

We were up at dawn, heading to the train station where we were planning to travel to a remote town in Andhra Pradesh. But before the train even arrived, I began to sense that Jennifer was ready for the lesson.

I had been preparing her for days. Taking her through some intense emotional processes to help her let go of her past.

I walked up to an old rusty metal post holding up a portion of the dilapidated roof of the train station.

I turned to Jennifer and said, "Jennifer, when you look at this post, what do you feel?"

She looked at me like I was crazy.

"I don't feel anything, Kute. It's just a metal post."

I nodded. "I know it is a post, Jennifer. But I want you to literally generate love for this post. Generate so much love for this post that your heart overflows with it. Love this post with the same intensity that you love your children."

She stood there, staring at the post, looking confused and frustrated.

"Kute, this is ridiculous. I can't generate anything. I can't love a dead post."

I looked at her and smiled. "Why don't you feel it? Why can't you feel it? What is stopping you from feeling love for this post?"

Jennifer huffed a sigh of frustration and pushed her hair out of her eyes. "I just don't feel anything!"

"Of course, I understand, Jennifer. This is just a post. But the post is a metaphor. It isn't about the post. I want you to realize that you have been conditioned to believe that something needs to occur for you to love something. That people need to love you first. That something needs to be guaranteed. But nothing needs to happen. The source of loving is not out there. Your capacity to love has nothing to do with anything out there."

She looked at me with a blank stare.

"Why can't you love this post? The post simply represents anything in your life that you are waiting to love. What I want you to understand is that right now you can love this post. It's your choice. See how you are holding back love. You tell yourself *I'm only going to love my daughter, I'm only going to love my husband, I'm only going to love my mother. I'm not going to love that person. I'm not going to love these strangers.* All of that love you are holding back already exists in your heart. What would happen if you gave it away? You don't need something out there to trigger it."

I paused.

"Where is the source of your love? Is it out there? No. That is an illusion. You are already love right now. It's your very nature. Your entire life has been spent trying to get people to love you *out there*, and you're still not happy. Right? You are love. It's in you. Nothing needs to happen and you don't need to be any different to access it. It is what you are."

Jennifer stared at me, her dark eyes filling with tears.

"Jennifer, it is what you ARE."

The tears started to course down her cheeks.

"Do you believe that?" I asked gently.

She nodded slowly.

"Good. So now there is no reason, if the love is inside you, if there is nothing that needs to be triggered, that you can't love this post right now. Open your heart. Feel the post. Sing to the post. Touch the post. There's no reason why you can't love this post. True freedom is the recognition that you are love. Then in all your relationships you can show up as that force. True love. It's what Gandhi did, it's what Mother Teresa did, it's what Martin Luther King did. That's why they were free in spite of their circumstances. They didn't need it, they were IT, and they knew it."

I paused.

"Free yourself right now. Why couldn't you love this thing right here?"

I watched as Jennifer turned and stared at the post. She reached out and touched the post, touched the cold metal, stared up at where it supported the heavy roof above. She then started to sing to it in a language I didn't understand, her native language, Russian. She began to dance around it, spinning and smiling in a kind of tribute of love to this post. The sun was now up, and people noticed her strange behavior and started gathering around to watch. I saw Jennifer become aware of the group and begin to falter in her actions. She almost stopped what she was doing.

I urged her on. "We are often afraid to love. What will people think? What will people say? What won't people say? What's going on out there has nothing, absolutely nothing, to do with your capacity to love now, in this moment. Mother Teresa herself said, 'Love is the reason for my life.' Can it be the reason for yours?"

Jennifer closed her eyes again. I couldn't hear the song now because of the noisy crowd that had gathered around us, but I felt it coming from her heart. "Your love has nothing to do with what you are loving. It's already in you. Is there any reason in your everyday life that you are not in touch with it? Why are you waiting for some event, some person, some feeling, to trigger it? Love for no reason. That is true freedom."

Soon she opened her eyes and turned to me, trembling. "Kute," she said, her voice tinged with awe, "you are right. I feel so much love right now. In my heart. For this . . . this post!" She chuckled.

I nodded.

"Okay, Jennifer, let's keep going. What else can you love more deeply in your life?"

We began to walk through the crowded station. As we walked, I pointed out different objects for her to love. A trash can. The newspapers. A tree. A piece of shit on the ground.

And every object was an invitation for Jennifer to love.

She offered it to each one. The level of love didn't change. Because it wasn't dependent on the object.

It was about what was in her heart. It was the overflow of her infinite spirit that was, in its essence, true love.

And then a beggar—a young girl—approached. She was dirty, smelly, and ragged. Her hair was unwashed and she had bruises all over her face.

She walked right up to Jennifer and looked her in the eyes.

I knew this could be a powerful moment.

"Jennifer, look into her eyes and open your heart. In this moment, feel the spark of the divine that is in her, that is in you. Get in touch with the reality that there's a life inside of her living. It is the same life in her that is in you. Feel that."

Jennifer started to weep as she looked into her eyes.

"She is your daughter. She is your mother. She is your sister," I said. "You want to know God, here she is, she's looking right back at you in the form of this girl. Feel that. There's God, right there. You want to be more spiritual, there she is right there. It's not about going to some temple and praising God.

"All of life is a gigantic temple. Everything in it is an expression of the divine. Everywhere you walk is holy ground.

"You walk around every day, Jennifer, in a church without walls. It's called the world. Each moment is an invitation, including this moment right now. You look at this woman and you think she's just a beggar; you look at her and you think she's just a wretched woman. Feel the formless essence. Feel through her to what's living, and you will know that there's only one of you here. She's here to remind you of who you are and who you've always been."

Jennifer reached out to the young girl and took her hand. She took her dirty hand and kissed it, and then she knelt down in front of her in reverence.

Every moment of your life is an invitation to love.

Can you love? Now?

Or do you hold back your love? Why do you hold back your love?

It is our nature to love.

Just like the awakening I had on my first trip to India, when I saw that woman in that train, and I saw how connected we all are as a people, as the human race. As you see how we are all one, we are all part of the divine, you no longer want to hold back love.

We are all living Buddhas.

The children in the orphanage. The beggar girl at the train station. Your ex-husband. Your in-laws.

When you change your view of love, when it is no longer dependent on someone's meeting a certain set of standards, you realize that you can love now. There is no more waiting. Now all those difficult relationships, where people don't measure up and keep annoying you, and you just wish things would go differently—they are invitations to practice love now.

You no longer have to suffer, wishing they were behaving differently.

Your mother-in-law, who tests your patience, gives you the opportunity to Love Now.

Changing diapers in the middle of the night when you're sleep deprived gives you an opportunity to Love Now.

The guy in front of you who cuts you off in traffic gives you an opportunity to Love Now.

Your impatient boss who screams at you gives you an opportunity to Love Now.

The rude valet parking attendant gives you an opportunity to Love Now.

Getting Real

I am not saying that the path of love is going to be easy from now on. It is a muscle you have to exercise. It is a daily choice that you must make.

When I returned from India, I thought daily of Dwarko-Ji and his challenge to love those children. But I didn't know how to love everyone yet. I didn't know how to treat those in front of me as living Buddhas. Every time I thought of Dwarko-Ji, I would ask myself: Right now, am I giving all of my love?

And I would have to admit, *No.*

Am I loving fully?

No.

Every time the answer was no.

After a few days, I got tired of that answer. So I tried to dig deeper. *Why not? Why aren't I choosing to love now?*

I would have to admit to myself: "I just don't feel like it right now."

As someone who was supposedly committed to the spiritual path, that was a painful admission. I was committed to exercising every day. I was committed to building my business.

But I was not really that committed to loving.

I began to see how easily I would shut down in relationships. A friend would do something to piss me off, and I would just walk away. I would cut them out of my life. I would be with my girlfriend and feel myself closing down my heart when she wasn't behaving the way I wanted her to. Instead of opening my heart and loving her, I would just shut down. My love was conditional.

And the more times I saw myself doing this, the more I recognized how much I had to learn.

So daily I would ask myself the question Could I love right now? Yes, I could. Yes, I could.

By admitting that I could love, I acknowledged what I was choosing. I began to see that I was actually REFUSING to love. Every moment I had it within my power to love. And I was refusing it.

I had never viewed love as a choice before. It was just something that either happened or didn't. It was a thing out there that sparked something in me.

But when you begin to see loving not as something that just happens but a commitment you make, a daily intentional practice to live, it takes on new meaning.

Love is not a feeling you have no control over, but a fierce commitment moment to moment.

So you have to admit to yourself: *Do I want to? No. Why not? I'm tired, I don't feel like it, that person doesn't deserve my love.* These are all excuses to hold back the one thing everyone in this world is craving more than life itself.

But I know there is another way. Begin to ask yourself the question daily: *Am I loving fully?* Or *Could I love right now*? This question becomes a kind of moment-to-moment meditation, and it can open your eyes to opportunities you may miss otherwise.

So when do you hold back? Do you hold back with your spouse? Do you expect him or her to meet a certain set of expectations and then you will offer your love?

Do you hold back with your siblings? Still harboring resentment from some inequality or injustice in the past?

Do you hold back with your coworkers? Your neighbors? Your kids?

Everyone that you meet is desperate for love. When you realize that love is something that can be shared with everyone, there is no limit to the love you can give.

Love is not a passive word. Love is not something to store high up on a shelf in your closet and bring out only on special occasions. Love is a living thing to be used every second of your life. Love is not just for the great saints and heroes of history. It is our birthright. Our destiny. Our responsibility. The more you use it, the more it grows. At the end of your life, the only thing you get to keep is the love you give away.

Gandhi was imprisoned many times throughout his life. But he never allowed feelings of anger, victimization, and hurt to overpower his call to love now. On one such occasion, after being imprisoned, Gandhi requested a pair of scissors and some leather and cloth from the prison warden. He was given these items, and during his stay in prison, he made a pair of sandals. He made them with great love and attention to detail.

Upon Gandhi's release from prison, he asked to see the army officer who had imprisoned him. He handed the sandals to the officer and said, "Officer, while in prison, I made these for you. A gift from me to you."

The officer was speechless.

Stunned into silence.

Gandhi simply turned around and walked out.

No words were necessary.

Even when staring injustice and cruelty in the face, we can choose to Love Now. It's easy to love when you get what you want. Life is kind to you. People are nice to you.

But it takes real courage to love when your life circumstances are difficult or unfair, and even greater courage when the people around you are unkind and rude.

But this is the invitation. This is when it really counts.

The True Spiritual Practice

If you find yourself saying, "Oh, well, only the great ones know how to love that unconditionally. They are special." That is an illusion.

If it was possible for Gandhi, it is possible for you. The great ones weren't special people with special powers. They were like you and me. They were simply examples of what was possible. They showed us our capacity to love and what we can all be. They simply dared to exercise their heart's capacity to love more and more.

To say THEY are the special ones is a cop-out. It is an excuse. If they are the special ones, then you don't have to step up and be THE ONE.

But just by being born YOU ARE THE ONE.

YOU ARE LOVE. And it's your nature to love.

This is the true spiritual practice. Opening your heart and sharing what is inside.

We often have so many ideas about what "being spiritual" is. You have to say the right words, do the right yoga postures, have the right altar, wear the right mala beads, burn the perfect incense, dress a certain kind of way, don't eat certain foods or hang out with only certain types of people—otherwise you're not spiritual.

That is a lie.

You can't *not* be spiritual.

You are spirit! So how could you not be spiritual? Pure spirit is the very foundation of each and every one of us! Black, white, rich, poor, saints and sinners—spirit is what we are made of. You cannot be anything else. Spiritual is not something you do; it's who you ARE inherently.

The only way you can be unspiritual is by denying your true nature.

I remember as a kid going to church every Sunday and watching everyone read scripture, sing, and worship. And yet right after church was over, people would be walking out the doors of the church, gossiping about one another. I remember asking my father about this, and he would simply smile and say, "Son, being spiritual is not what you do in church on a Sunday, it's how you live the other six days of your life. Church isn't simply a place you visit once a week. It's a state of consciousness in your heart. Then every moment of your life becomes spiritual."

I once heard the story of Mumtaz, a devout Muslim woman. All her life she dreamed of making the pilgrimage to Mecca. The journey to Mecca is a religious duty that must be carried out by every able-bodied Muslim who is able to do so at least once in his or her lifetime. Mumtaz worked as a maid and earned very little money, but she always saved a little bit toward her pilgrimage. She stashed away her cash underneath her mattress for over thirty years.

One day, just a few days before the pilgrimage season was beginning, when she counted up all her savings, she realized that she finally had enough money to make the pilgrimage to Mecca. She rejoiced and began to pack a small bag. As she locked up the door of her apartment, finally ready to go to the train station, she noticed a foul smell lingering in the air.

"What is that smell?" she wondered as she followed the scent to her neighbor's door.

She knocked on the door, and when her neighbor answered, she said, "Is everything okay?"

"We are boiling leaves to make soup for dinner," the wife explained with a shy look.

Upon seeing the leaves in the pot, Mumtaz knew they were deadly. "Those leaves are poisonous!" she warned. "And if you eat them you're going to die!"

"We will die anyway. We have no food," said the husband.

Mumtaz looked at her neighbors in shock. Her neighbors were literally starving. Mumtaz reached into her bag and pulled out the envelope that held her life savings. She placed it in her neighbor's hands.

"Here," she said. "Take this. Consider it a gift from God."

And she excused herself, returned to her home, and began the next day once again saving for her pilgrimage to Mecca.

When pilgrimage season ended, the angels in the heavens reviewed the different pilgrims who had traveled to Mecca.

"Who had the greatest pilgrimage?" they began to ask.

"Maybe it was this one who traveled the greatest distance?" an angel said.

"It could have been this one who spent the most money," another offered.

This debate among the angels went on for a while.

"No!" another angel said. "It was Mumtaz!"

"Mumtaz?" the angels cried out. "She didn't even go to Mecca."

"Ahhhh, but she did," said the angel. "She made the greatest pilgrimage in her heart!"

Like Mumtaz, you do not need to go anywhere.

If you find yourself thinking, *Oh, if only I could go to India with Kute! Then I could truly transform! Then I could start really living my life!*

Let me say it again. You do not need to go anywhere.

You do not need to go to India or Bali.

This moment holds the power to change your life.

This is the spiritual practice. Discovering how to make everything you do a sacred act. In the middle of the marketplace. In the middle of chaos. In the midst of life.

The bottom line of practicing any religion or walking any spiritual path is the degree to which you are able to love.

The Most Important Choice of Your Life

I learned this firsthand by example when I was walking the Camino de Santiago. I spent most of that journey by myself. That was part of the point. To be with my thoughts. To meditate on my life.

About twenty days into my journey, I entered a small monastery to stay the night. In the kitchen, a small group of travelers sat around a table. One man was chopping up food and sharing it with the group. He was laughing and seemed at ease, as if he belonged there. "Come in," he said with a smile. "Would you like to have a seat?"

"Sure," I said, thankful to rest my feet for a while. "Are you in charge?"

He smiled and shook his head. "No, I'm not," he said. "My name is Eduardo. But please, join us for dinner." I joined the small band of fellow pilgrims and soon found myself enjoying a delicious meal and entertaining stories, thanks to Eduardo.

The next day Eduardo and I decided to walk together. Up until this point, I had walked the Camino alone. But on this day, something guided me to walk with this man. I knew that today I would face one of the most challenging stretches of the journey, a hike straight uphill sixteen miles into high elevation. It would be nice to have some company.

As we walked, Eduardo made jokes to lighten the mood on the tough trek. Each step we took got harder, and I soon found myself focusing on Eduardo's backpack. It was one of those large backpacker backpacks. And you could tell it was jampacked. It must have weighed about forty pounds.

Why does he need all of that stuff? I wondered.

Soon we began to discuss what had brought us to the Camino.

"Well, Kute," he said, "my wife recently left me for another man."

I looked at him in shock. In his circumstances, I would have been a basket case. And yet here was this man laughing, joking, smiling. He was one of the most carefree people I had seen on the trail thus far. I never would have guessed the heartbreak that must have been dwelling within.

"How are you managing?" I asked.

"I don't own her," he said humbly. "I don't possess her. If I truly love her, I must set her free. And if it's meant to be, she'll come back to me. I want her to be with me because she's inspired out of love, not because of an ultimatum or out of obligation. I'm not her jailer and love is not a prison. If my wife and I can be in a relationship together as an expression of our love and freedom, then that's what I want. I don't want her to love me out of obligation."

"Wow," I said, amazed. "That must be hard! How do you not hold on to bitterness or anger toward her?" I asked.

"Well, what do you mean when you say the words I LOVE YOU?" Eduardo asked. "Often what we mean is I want you to be mine and do what I say. But real love is unconditional. We are all souls on a journey of life. We have our own lessons to learn. Unconditional love supports each person's soul's journey. Even if it doesn't match yours at this time. Trying to make someone be what you want him or her to be isn't love. It's a form of manipulation."

We paused at the top of a difficult hill and Eduardo took a drink of water. I stared at this man. "When you love unconditionally, Kute, you are free. This is my path, and this is why I walk the Camino each day. Anyone can say I LOVE YOU, but the real journey is to live love. I've walked the Camino seven times from beginning to end. This is my eighth time," he announced.

Eduardo paused again. The path reached straight up ahead of us. He turned to look at me.

"This time my commitment is to no longer walk for myself. My commitment is to be of service and love others on the journey. I'm walking for you . . . and for all of the pilgrims who feel a call in their heart to walk."

He paused.

"I'm just here to be love on the journey of life."

I looked at this man. At his kind face full of compassion. At the laugh lines around his eyes. Here I was on the Camino, thinking I knew something about what it means to live a spiritual life. Eduardo showed me how far I still had to go.

We continued to walk, now up the steep embankment in front of us. All I could see was the rocky path in front of me and Eduardo's enormous backpack.

So I asked the question that had been on my mind from the start. "So, Eduardo, what is it you carry in that backpack, man? I thought the journey on the Camino was about letting go," I said with a soft laugh, sort of mocking him.

He turned back and smiled at me. "Nothing in this backpack is for me," he said. "It's filled with gifts of love for those who walk the journey with me. And my goal is that by the end of the journey, my backpack will be completely empty. I walk to give everything I have away. Nothing in my backpack belongs to me. Dare to give everything you have," he said to me. "And at the end of your life, make sure there's no love left behind inside of your heart."

Boom!

I followed in his footsteps the rest of that day, knowing that I was walking in the wake of a great man. A man who knew what life was really all about. We talked about my life, about where I came from, and about my struggle to find my way out of my father's shadow. About my mom back home in London and how much I missed her, but how much I appreciated her support and faith in me. She was my own picture of unconditional love.

We made our way slowly that day. Some of it was the strenuousness of the path, but we also spent time handing out Eduardo's gifts. Every time we met someone on the path, Eduardo would pull something from his backpack to share—an apple, a coin, a postcard—with that traveler.

Twelve hours later, we reached our destination for the night. I went to bed, sadly realizing that in the morning Eduardo and I would go our separate ways.

That night he came to my room. "Kute, I have a gift for you. I wrapped this before I came and I didn't know why. But I'd like you to give this to your mother so she can know more about the Camino journey. Open this tomorrow morning before you start walking," he instructed.

"Thank you," I said, and I meant it for so much more than the gift. We hugged and said goodbye.

As I began walking the next day, I suddenly remembered the package. I ripped through the wrapping paper and discovered an old book about the Camino written entirely in Japanese! There was a card attached with a handwritten note. It said simply, *I Love You*.

I stood there on the path, holding this book that was meant for my mother. Clearly the universe had known that I would meet Eduardo. And in his pack, he had been carrying this unique, special gift, that would really mean something only to me.

He taught me that everyone is our family. Love is our language.

Eduardo revealed the power of Love Now.

He wasn't withholding love from his wife after she betrayed him. He still loved her and offered her that love. His love for her was not dependent on her actions.

Even more shocking for me was that he was walking the Camino and offering love to everyone on the trail. Not just the people he liked. Not simply those people who were kind to him.

Every single person on the trail was an invitation for him to love.

What would our world look like if we could all live like Eduardo? Fully committed every day to leaving nothing in our backpack?

This is our calling. This is our spiritual practice.

To finally realize that you are love, that you have no reason to hold it back, is the moment that you become truly free.

Free to love. Free to risk. Free to be who you truly are.

YOU are love.

Don't wait for "the one" to say the three most powerful words.

YOU. ARE. THE. ONE.

You are love. You were born to love. Everyone is waiting for your love. What else is there to do but Love Now?

CONCLUSION

THE REAL JOURNEY BEGINS

This is not the end.

This is just the beginning.

We have peeled the layers. Why?

We peel the layers to set you free. Free to love. Free to live. Free to give. Free to be yourself fully.

We peel the layers so that you can rediscover what you have inside you that has been waiting to be brought to light. So you can finally understand that inside you is a mighty power that the world desperately needs.

Never underestimate what's possible when a human being makes a decision.

To rise up.

To surrender.

To step into the game.

The Power of One Banana

On Clark's last day in India, I took him back to the train station.

Some of our greatest moments had been here, in this crowded station, filled with humanity. So Clark knew the drill. Something was going to happen.

But as we weaved through the crowds, I saw a sadness descend upon him as he looked at the many children with no place to lay their heads. The beggars, their eyes full of hope and hunger. And as we walked, he spoke up. "Kute, I don't understand how you do it. How you come here, trip after trip, and see this poverty. How does it not break your heart? I mean, as I get ready to go back home, all I can think is what can anyone do to help? What can one really do? I mean, I try and give to charity, but to help all these people—you would just need millions of dollars to make a difference. There is just so much need."

He shook his head in defeat.

Now, let me remind you. Clark was a rich man. He had countless resources.

It wasn't about getting more resources.

So I left Clark sitting in the train station. I went to a nearby market and bought four bags filled with bananas. It cost me five dollars. I walked back to Clark and led him to the bridge that overlooks the train station.

Underneath the bridge was an encampment of homeless families sprawled across the pavement. Every time I have visited India, there have been homeless people living here. The faces change, but the place doesn't. They sleep under the bridge at night. During the day, they beg on the bridge teeming with tourists trying to get to the train station.

"Clark, I know you feel the pain and suffering of these people. And that is good. But it is time to see how much you have to give. I want you to go down there, to those men, women, and children who have nothing. And I want you to give each of them a banana. I know a banana may not seem like much. But I want you to give each banana as if it contained all of your love and compassion. Pour all of the compassion that you feel right now in your heart into each banana you give."

Clark took the heavy bags. He stumbled down the hill and began to walk through the group of homeless people, handing out bananas.

Within seconds, dozens of people swarmed him. Young and old, they all came. Children. Handicapped. Women with babies in their arms. One by one he gave them each a banana. Once he had no more bananas, they didn't push him away; they brought him into their community. They sang and danced with him.

I stood on the side of the bridge and watched the joy emanating from their faces.

And none more than Clark's.

After an hour, I went down to get Clark. It took a while to pull him away from his new crowd of friends. Some of the children followed us up the hill as we sat on the top of the bridge, our legs dangling as we looked down at his new friends still buzzing with excitement. As if they had just won the lottery.

I looked at Clark. Tears were streaming down his face.

"What is it, Clark?"

He shook his head. He was crying too hard to speak.

"It wasn't about how much I could give," he finally managed to say. "It was just about seeing them and being willing to do one simple thing. I wouldn't have thought that just one banana . . ." He paused as he tried to control his emotions. "I wouldn't have thought that one banana would have made a difference. But it did. It did. And then once my pockets were empty, I literally had nothing to give them. But something switched for me in that moment. I realized I have my heart. I have the love in my heart! I can give them that, even though I didn't have anything tangible to offer. And you know what? That's all they wanted! It was more powerful than anything else I could have given."

I nodded. "Yes, it is powerful to see how many times we pass people by, thinking we can't do enough, when we can just do one simple thing that can mean the world."

We sat there in silence. In some ways this was a culmination of all the lessons we had learned in India. Clark had discovered his power. He had discovered that in every moment of his life, he can be open to what is seeking to happen through him. He saw how powerful it can be to finally be available to Love Now. At any moment he could give a banana or he could give a dollar. He could do a dance or he could sing a song.

It wasn't about what he was doing. It was about who he was being. It was about the love he was offering. It was about him sharing his gift with the world.

You simply being your authentic self fully is the greatest gift you can give the world.

Clark took a deep breath, staring up into the blue sky, the crowded traffic of India blaring around us. Then he spoke again.

"When I'm in America, I can write a check and be done with it and think I'm actually serving people. But so often, truly, it doesn't mean anything. It is an empty check, and I move on, being untouched, closed off. While I was here, you took everything from me. I had nothing to give other than myself, other than my heart, who I was. So I had to dig deeper. I couldn't just avoid anymore, and it took me to a place deep inside myself."

We started to walk back toward the train station, a parade of children following us.

"We all have something to give, no matter what. The most important thing is the love we give. I see in my life that I've received what I thought was love from people by buying them things, doing things for them, giving them money. That's how I learned to get love. It had been a trade. That's part of what has driven me to be successful in my life. The more successful I was, the more I could buy people off. Then they would love me. My greatest fear has been failure, to have nothing, because then I thought I would never be loved."

He paused and looked around at the children who were still trailing us. "Yet here I am with nothing. And it took me beyond that fear. Here it was clear that I could just love these people, and they loved me back. Something just clicked for me. I feel free. I feel totally free now. Because I know that I have so much to offer the world, just being who I am."

I nodded, smiling ear to ear. "Now, Clark, you have become the richest man in the world."

And that right there is the journey.

The point of peeling the layers is to realize all that you have within. You no longer live in the shell of a persona. You no longer live in the prison of your conditioning. You no longer let your mind limit you. You no longer cling to control as the answer to your problems. You no longer hold back love, the one thing our world is starving for.

You realize that you have everything you need. Like the man at the beginning of this book. You can sing your song fully, knowing it is the only thing you need to do.

Starting the Rest of Your Life

My last day with a client is always bittersweet. They have come so far from when they stepped on the plane fourteen days earlier, an unhappy, trapped person desperate for me to give them any information about where they are going or what we are doing.

As for Clark, he was preparing to go back to his life. But his previous life was set up for a tiny, quiet mouse. And he was returning as a big, loud, powerful lion.

As we drove to the airport, I had him write letters to all his loved ones again. This time, the letters were about the changes that had occurred in India. In many ways he was reintroducing himself to his family. Not as who he'd been for forty-five years. But as who he truly was.

I then handed him an MP3 player that held recordings from his family, who had taped messages for him before he left. He sat in the back of the car weeping as he heard the voices of his wife and children and the prayers they had for him on the journey. And he knew, deep in his heart, that their prayers had been answered.

We arrived at the airport and checked in for our different flights. We would not be flying home together. So this was it. It was time to say goodbye.

We stood in the atrium of the airport in Bombay, looking into each other's eyes. We couldn't have been more different. But we had shared this journey. And we knew deep down we were the same.

I handed him back his passport, his cell phone, and his wallet.

"You're free to have your life now. Enjoy it."

He looked at me with tears in his eyes. This was about more than the passport. He knew that he was truly being given another chance at life.

"I love you, man," he said quietly, looking down.

"I love you, too," I said with a smile. "Come here," I said, laughing, and I pulled him into a big bear hug.

When we pulled apart, I said, "I have one more surprise for you."

This time he didn't know what to expect.

I handed him his ticket.

He looked at it. And realized that it said first class.

He stood there in shock. "I'm flying first class?"

I nodded.

"You are not the same person you came here as. When you truly surrender, you are free to have first class, to have a wife and kids, to have whatever material success befalls you because it no longer owns you. You no longer need it. People think that surrender is about renouncing things. It's not about renouncing things. It's about having the right relationship with them. When you no longer *need* it, then you are free to have it. Without it having you. You no longer need first class to feel free. You are freedom!"

Clark shook his head, still in shock.

"Thank you," he said again.

"You're welcome," I said. "Okay, go on then. Enjoy your life! I love you! The force is with you!"

Clark turned to go.

And walked off to start the rest of his life.

Your Invitation to an Epic Life

If you feel like you have been holding back who you truly are, the time has come to stop. Holding back your gifts is painful. It is time, now that you have peeled back the layers, to let your power out.

Stop holding back. Searching for your purpose. Or what you are supposed to do with your life.

Looking for your life purpose is like a fish in the ocean looking for water.

It's all around you. Just waiting for you to claim it.

I hope by now you realize that an epic life isn't reserved for only a select few. Spielberg. Oprah. Mandela. Gandhi. Zuckerberg. Jobs.

But it is a birthright for you and me.

So if you are waiting for a sign, the fact that you are alive is the very sign you are waiting for. The fact that you are reading this book means you are ready.

Your gifts aren't simply your gifts.

They don't just belong to you. They belong to the universe.

They belong to all of humanity. Everyone is called. Everyone is chosen.

Not everyone says YES to the calling.

Jesus. Buddha. MLK. Mother Teresa. They said yes. They reached for the stars not just for themselves, but to inspire *you*. They have opened the door and shown you what is possible. Jesus himself said, "The things I do greater than these can you also do."

I grew up in a church. So take it from me. It's time to stop worshiping the great ones. That's right. Stop worshiping Jesus. Worshiping the Buddha. Worshiping Gandhi. For too long we have worshiped them as if they alone were special.

You are the one. Which means you too have inside you the potential to be a great one. We are called not to worship the great ones, but to LIVE their message. Embody it. Even Gandhi himself said, "When I die, burn my books in my cremation." He didn't want to be worshiped. He wanted people to follow his example. That is the only kind of worship that matters.

When the great ones saw the trouble brewing in our world, they did not allow their hearts to fill with despair. They saw those challenges as an invitation to step up. A call to give of their love. Practice their compassion. Be who they truly were.

This is your invitation, too.

You too were born to have an epic life. To do things with such great love that they are talked about for generations.

You were not born to crawl the valleys but to fly the skies.

So as I hand you back your passport, know that you have within you everything you seek. Everything the world needs.

You are the richest person in the world.

YOU. ARE. THE. ONE.

ACKNOWLEDGMENTS

When I think of everyone who has contributed to bringing this book to life, no words can adequately express my deep gratitude for the incredible support from so many people.

This book is the sum total of every single person who has ever touched my life. It has been a true collaboration and labor of love of so many amazing souls. My heartfelt appreciation to each of you.

I do, however, wish to thank certain people who have not only helped birth this book but who also have been there for me.

First, deepest gratitude to my publisher, Michele Martin. From the first moment we met you believed in me and my work. Thank you for your unwavering commitment to this book being great.

Also, a big thank you to the amazing team at North Star Way/Simon & Schuster: Kathy Huck, Sophia Muthuraj for your editorial support; Hilary Mau for all your hard work; Cindy Ratzlaff for your publishing expertise; cover designers John Vairo, Jr., and Emma Van Deun; production editor Navorn Johnson; publicist Melissa Gramstad; interior designers Davina Mock and Renato Stanisic; and managing editors Irene Kheradi and Amanda Mulholland.

To Cindy Di Tiberio, for helping me bring my message to life in book form. You were a true partner in the process. Your countless hours of brainstorming, brilliant editing skills, encouragement, and commitment have made this book what it is. It has been a joy working with you.

A big thanks to Darnella Ford for your help in organizing and editing my ideas during the initial stages of writing, long before there was a manuscript.

To both of my agents at WME. Eric Rovner, I will never forget that meeting in your office. I appreciate your belief in me and in my work reaching a broader audience. It's just the beginning. And my book agent, Eric Lupfer, thanks for always showing up and for shepherding the book into the world.

To my amazing team at The Blackson Group. My right-hand man, Cesar Franco. Your dedication and service to the mission of transforming lives is deeply inspiring. My deep love and gratitude for all that you are. And to Heather Godfrey, for your love and pure spirit of service. I am blessed for your support and for all you do each day to spread the message of love to the world.

To all the amazing people whom I have had the privilege of coaching one on one, and that have ever attended one of my events, or supported my work. You have all helped to write this book and have given me so much.

Thank you to all the early inspirations who impacted me as a young boy. You have all paved the way for me to be here—J Krishnamurti, Ernest Holmes, Osho, Maharishi Mahesh Yogi, Charles Fillmore, Ramana Maharisi, Stuart Wilde, Louise Hay, Wayne Dyer, Jack Canfield, Marianne Williamson, Tony Robbins, Barbara De Angelis, Emmet Fox, Swami Muktananda, VV Brahmam, and many more.

To my dear friends, thank you for understanding and loving me. Gina Cloud, your friendship and unconditional love is beyond words. Matthew and Deborah Mitchell, you are always there when I need you. Arielle Ford and Brian Hilliard, thank you for taking me into your hearts and supporting me like a brother! Jeannie Kang, thank you for your kindness throughout the years. Christine Hassler, thank you for trusting your intuition and making the book connection! To my soul sister Ida Resi Alit, I am blessed by your love and friendship.

To my PR team at Krupp Kommunications. Caity Cudworth, Jennifer Garbowski, Stephen Schonberg, Megan Miller, and Heidi Krupp-Lisiten. Thanks for your belief in my work and commitment to spreading it to the world!

Last but not least to my dear parents. Much of who I am is influenced by you. You showed me the real meaning of a life of service, and living each day dedicated to love. I am eternally grateful to your souls.